HEYDRICH
HENCHMAN OF DEATH

HEYDRICH
HENCHMAN OF DEATH

by

CHARLES WHITING

LEO COOPER

First published in Great Britain in 1999, Reprinted 1999 by
LEO COOPER
an imprint of
Pen & Sword Books Ltd
47 Church Street
Barnsley
South Yorkshire
S70 2AS

ISBN 0 85052 629 9

A catalogue record for this book is
available from the British Library

Typeset in 11/13pt Candida
by Phoenix Typesetting, Ilkley, West Yorkshire

Printed in England by Redwood Books Ltd,
Trowbridge, Wilts

CONTENTS

ACKNOWLEDGMENTS

I should like to thank the following for their help with this book: My friend and fellow author Eric Taylor (York); writer-editor Wolfgang Trees (Aachen); the widow of Reinhard Heydrich and her family; Tom Dickinson (New York).

Charles Whiting

PREFACE

A forty-minute journey on a little train that winds through snow-capped mountains brings you to the place. It looks very shabby and rundown for a supposed tourist resort. The tunnel under the main line stinks of urine and the walls are covered with Neo-Nazi graffiti. There are drunks outside the travel bureau (closed), which was once the VIP waiting room. The kiosk sells soft porn, Bavarian beer and Turkish papers to frightened-looking workers. Yet once this rural Bavarian station had been, perhaps, the most important in the world. Kings and princes had once descended here from their luxury trains to be greeted by stiff, black-uniformed guardsmen. They had come from all over the world to pay homage, while high above them, two thousand feet or more, the new master of Europe, Adolf Hitler, waited for them.

Back in 1924 Hitler himself had first arrived at Berchtesgaden station. Then he had been a jailbird, just released from Landsberg Prison after his abortive Munich Putsch of 1923. He had been at a loose end. His new party was in disarray. He was broke and had been forbidden to speak in public for the next three years. He headed straight up the mountain opposite the station to meet a certain, possibly half-mad, Dieter Eckart, anti-semite, drug addict, rabble-rouser, crackpot 'philosopher' – and a founder member of the German Workers' Party, which had been the brief forerunner of Hitler's new *Nationalsozialistiche Deutsche Arbeiter* (Nazi) Party.

Eckart filled the young Austrian's head with his crazy ideas of German racial purity. More importantly, he introduced Hitler to Munich's high society and those representatives of German Big Business, Flick, Mercedes, Siemens, Krupp and the like, the same firms which supply us with cars, fridges, washing machines, and banking services to this very day. They were to become the people who would finance the Nazi Party in years to come.

Eckart is buried half a mile away, in Berchtesgaden's town cemetery. Nearby, in the *Burgfriedhof* (Mountain Cemetery) overlooking the little station, Paula Hitler, the Führer's half-sister, is buried, as is Dr Fritz Todt, the engineer who built the autobahns and the Siegfried Line.

During the thirties all the *Prominenten* of the Third Reich visited 'Hitler's Mountain', as it was called at the time. Some even had their own houses on the heights above the *Kehlberg*. Like Mafia bosses, they thought it wise to be as close as possible to their 'Don' at all times. Martin Bormann, Hitler's 'Brown Eminence', built a house there, as did Albert Speer, his architect, and Hermann Goering, who boasted that if a single British bomb fell on the Reich he would be called 'Meyer' (a supposed Jewish name). Today, just outside what is left of his house, are three bomb craters made by the RAF.

But of all the leading Nazis, perhaps the most evil of the lot only rode up the mountain to see his Führer once, and even then he came only as second-in-command to his boss, *Reichsführer der SS* Heinrich Himmler. He was tall and blond, high-cheeked in the fashion of those Germans born in the East who have Slavic blood. Arrogant, haughty and cold-eyed, he seemed to put the fear of death into all with whom he had dealings. Even Hitler appeared a little afraid of him. Hitler said of him, privately, after that first meeting: 'He is a man with an iron heart'. And Hitler didn't make such remarks about his followers lightly.

This thirty-four-year-old black-clad officer was Reinhard Tristan Heydrich. Then unknown outside Party circles, he has remained to some extent unknown ever since. We have very few descriptions of him, though Hitler's second-in-command, Walter Schellenberg, did write of him after the war: 'He was a tall impressive figure with a broad, unusually high forehead, small restless eyes as crafty as an animal's and of uncanny power. . . . His splendid figure was marred by the breadth of his hips, a disturbingly feminine effect which made him appear even more sinister.'

Pierre Huss, who is supposed to have known him well, states that 'Heydrich had a mind and mentality like an adding machine, never forgetting or lapsing into the sentimental . . . nobody ever got a break or consideration of mercy.' His wife, on the other hand, thought that he had 'beautiful fingers' and said she would 'have never married if he hadn't come to woo her with his violin'.

The world, in so far as it remembers this sinister figure at all, remembers him as the 'Father of the Final Solution', who was rightly murdered on the orders of . . . and that is the question. Of whom? The Czechs? The British and the Czechs? Possibly even the British Royal Family, because he knew too much about the Duke of Windsor's supposed links with Hitler.

It is here that the mysteries connected with Heydrich begin, but do not end. Why did his brother Thomas volunteer for the Russian front, where he disappeared after reading the documents passed on to him after his brother's death? Why was Heydrich's widow protected by the British SIS? Who tried to burn down her house on the remote island to which she had fled in a kind of self-imposed exile? Why does Thomas Heydrich, his nephew, appear all over North Germany in little theatres and village schools, singing songs in, of all languages, Yiddish? Heydrich must be spinning in his grave, wherever that is – yet another mystery.

But the greatest mystery of all is one that reaches right into our own time. *It is that 'golden link' between Heydrich's SS 'Economic Empire' and the New Europe of the Year 2000.* This book is a modest attempt to solve some of these mysteries.

I

TO START A WAR

In starting a war, it is not *right* that
matters, but victory.

Adolf Hitler, August, 1939

1

The man who was to start the Second World War was sweating, but it wasn't just the unusually sticky heat of that August evening in 1939. As he drove his big open tourer through the Nollendorfplatz and then through the Potsdamerstrasse, heading for the Reich Security Headquarters in the Prinz-Albrecht Palais, he was worried about the reason for his hasty summons to see the 'Old Man'. Why had he been called out at this time of the evening, long after duty hours, and in such great haste? He was always worried when the 'Old Man' wanted to see him out of hours, and a bit scared as well.

A few minutes earlier he had been about to leave his apartment when the special phone which connected him directly with headquarters rang. As he recalled years later: 'Firstly, there was seldom anything good that came to me over that phone. Secondly, I had a date with a new girl friend.' But there would be no time for new girl friends that night or for many to come. He picked up the phone and a voice at the other end snapped, 'Adjutant's office here,' – ('my office,' he thought, although the voice at the other end was unfamiliar) – 'Please come to the Old Man's office as quickly as possible. Please be here in twenty minutes. *Heil Hitler*.' And that had been that.

His name was Alfred Naujocks, formerly a student of engineering at the University of Kiel. In those days students still wore the white cap and colours of the student society to which they belonged and carried a cane. But there was nothing effete about Naujocks. In the hungry early thirties, with the 'Browns' and the 'Reds' actively engaged in street battles, he had been in the forefront of the brown-shirted attack on the 'Reds'. In a series of roughhouses with communist students and their supporters, the tough Kiel dockworkers, he had managed to get his nose broken twice. Indeed he often said that he should have been given the 'Blood Order' awarded to those of the pre-1933 Party faithful who had shed their blood for Adolf Hitler and the National Socialist German Workers' Party. But even when he did reach the rank of Colonel, before wisely deserting to the British in 1944, he never received much in the way of decorations. In his kind of work it wasn't thought advisable by the authorities that his deeds should be advertised.

Naujocks had joined the SS in 1931, at a time when its head, Heinrich Himmler, was trying to attract a better class of recruit than the workers who had formed the nucleus of Hitler's Storm Troopers, the Party's original bullyboys. Naujocks thought he fitted the bill perfectly. He had passed the *Abitur* (the German High School Leaving Certificate, necessary to go to university or become an officer) and, although he was studying engineering, he had intellectual pretensions, reading history and philosophy as his preferred subjects.

Four years later Naujocks transferred from the *Allgemeine SS* to the *Sicherheitsdienst (SD)*, the SS's own security and spy organization. To his chagrin, he found that the *SD*, and in particular its youthful head, known behind his back as *der Alte* (the Old Man), was not interested in his intellectual pretensions, but rather in the size of his biceps, the quickness of his physical reactions and his ability to use a silenced pistol. So Naujocks became, over the next few years, what the American author William L. Shirer has called in his monumental *Rise and Fall of the Third Reich* 'a sort of intellectual gangster', who could be relied upon to carry out any unsavoury secret mission needing both brawn and brain.

He had stage-managed a revolt in Slovakia, whose people felt they weren't fully represented in the Czechoslovakian union. This was the start of Hitler's attempts to put pressure on that country on Germany's south-eastern border before the final take-over. Naujocks 'disposed' of an exiled German Social Democrat who was running an irritating propaganda

2

radio station directed at the Reich from the Czech capital of Prague. He helped to set up the senior Russian Army commander, Marshal Tukhachevsky, making it appear to the Russian dictator, Stalin, that the former had been bribed by the Germans to work in their interests. As a result the Marshal and 35,000 other key Russian officers had been liquidated by the time Germany invaded the Soviet Union in 1941. Most of the 'money' he used for bribes was produced by German forgers imprisoned in Nazi Concentration Camps, but neither the 'Old Man' nor Stalin worried about such trivialities.

By the later thirties Naujocks, whose main interests were skirt-chasing, airy philosophizing about his country's role in history and, more reluctantly, violence, had been involved in half a dozen clandestine operations of which he was inordinately proud. Indeed among his friends and colleagues he was now calling himself *des Führer's Meisteragent* (the Führer's Master Agent).

But on this sticky August evening Naujocks could never have guessed the importance of the mission he was soon to undertake. Its completion would involve the Third Reich in a war that would change the face of Europe, leave the Continent stricken and ruined for nearly a decade and cost the lives of at least thirty million people.

At the top of the steps leading to the Security Police HQ in Prinz-Albrecht Palais the two black-clad guards of the *Leibstandarte* clicked to attention. Naujocks acknowledged their salute with a nod and hurried inside the building. He passed on to the waiting room outside the Old Man's office and was surprised to find that it wasn't empty. Two other officers were already there. They were Heinrich 'Heini' Müller, who would go down in the history of that infamous organisation as 'Gestapo' Müller, and Arthur Nebe, another ex-cop, now the head of the *Kripo*, the Criminal Investigation Police. Naujocks liked neither of them, nor did they like him; to them he was a new boy, untrained in real police work. All the same they replied promptly enough to his greeting, as he clicked to attention and barked 'Heil Hitler.' It was wise to do so, even for senior men like themselves. Müller, a former Bavarian policeman, looked up, but said nothing. Nebe, one day to be

3

hunted for his life by the very man now sitting next to him, exclaimed, 'What, you here too, Naujocks?'

Naujocks smiled, but said nothing. But, as he recalled later, 'It did me good to see the two of them nervous, especially the mighty Gestapo Müller, who usually knew everything that was going on. But it was always the same. Those who were closest to the Old Man were the most afraid of him.'

Then the green light above the Old Man's door started to blink on and off, and the three of them sprang to their feet. An officer appeared as if from nowhere, wearing the immaculate black uniform of the SS with the silver marking of the feared SD on his arm. '*Der Gruppenführer lasst bitten,*' he announced, clicking the heels of his polished jackboots together, and they went through into the Old Man's office. It had started.

2

It was the singer's fate that he lived in a region and at a time where anti-semitism was well established. Despite the fact that his wife was a staunch Catholic and he himself was a great admirer of Wagner, whose Germanic philosophy and belief that the Jews presented a danger to the purity of the Teutonic race he supported, all his life he himself was regarded as a Jew.

Bruno, for that was the singer's name, didn't look particularly Jewish, but he was not helped by the fact that in his performances he would slip into the role of what locals called an *Isidor*, the caricature of a Jew. As one resident of the Saxon city of Halle, in which Bruno spent most of his professional life, recalled, 'most of the inhabitants had not the slightest doubt about his Jewish origin.'

Naturally, among the bourgeois worthies to whom Bruno belonged by profession and status, it didn't help that, after the death of his father, his mother had taken a second husband, a locksmith with the unfortunate name of Suess. Everyone knew that Suess was a Jewish name.

We do not know how Bruno Suess-Heydrich (for that was his official name) felt about his supposed Jewishness. Outwardly he seemed to make a joke of the matter. But for our purposes it is not important what he did or did not feel. What is important is the impact it had on Bruno's second son, born in Halle on 7 March, 1904.

He was christened Reinhard Tristan after Wagner's opera *Tristan and Isolde*, but as he grew up he appeared, with his blond hair and clear blue eyes, to fit the stereotype of the Nordic hero.

'Reini', as he was nicknamed, was also intended for a musical career. Although he was regarded by the family as a quiet, well-behaved boy, he could at times be awkward. He was something of an outsider who always knew best and, when he thought it important, firmly stood up for his rights.

But although his appearance was ideally Nordic, he was handicapped by a squeaky, high-pitched voice which earned him the nickname of *Ziege* (Billy-goat) among his contemporaries. To make matters worse, his father's supposed Jewish origin had followed him to high school, where he was known by the soubriquet which dogged him for the rest of his life – Izzy. For, despite all the genealogical research later carried out on his behalf, he always believed, in fact mistakenly, that he was one quarter Jewish.[*]

Heydrich soon realized that he was not going to fit in at school. He wasn't interested in athletics, though he later achieved national status as a fencer. He was burdened by his falsetto voice and fat girlish hips and there was the problem of his being thought to be Jewish. He knew that if he didn't want to be treated as a worm for the rest of his life he would have to be tougher, crueller, bolder, more ambitious, more powerful than all the rest. So he set out to toughen himself up and create for himself the air of being superior to any of his schoolmates.

He took to walking alone to and from school. He walked along the curb, one foot on the pavement, one in the gutter. He never deflected from his course, even for adults. Generally, people got out of his way when they saw him coming, for he had quickly achieved a reputation for aggressiveness. But if anyone challenged his right to continue on his course, then it would come to a fight, into which he threw himself with reckless abandon.

[*] Most adult Germans of that period had to prove that there was no Jewish blood in their family as far back as 1760.

6

He also began showing off. Once he climbed on the school roof, three floors above the school yard sixty feet or more below. There, in full view of the horrified staff, he made his way along the gutter. The slightest slip would have sent him to his death below!*

When he joined the navy in March, 1922, he found an outlet for his aggressiveness in fencing. But on his first home leave he was still greeted by the mocking cries of his former schoolmates: 'Look, there's Izzy Suess in naval uniform'. It rankled, but, as he told his brother, 'There's nothing I can do about it,' which was true. Even his classmates of 'Crew 22', as his year was called, had rejected him. His sense of isolation grew ever deeper.

But as he grew older he became, not only a champion fencer, but also a *Weiberheld* (a womanizer). The great sexual swordsman was not particular. He chased them all with unrelenting zeal, whore and virgin, working class or high-born lady. The whores he encountered on his overseas cruises were all the same to him. He took them either with money or by force, and left them as soon as he had his way. But eventually his relentless search for sex caught up with him. In 1931 he was called before a court of honour to answer to a charge of 'conduct unbecoming to a gentleman and an officer of the German Navy'. The year before he had become officially engaged to Lina von Osten, who, despite her aristocratic name, was the daughter of a primary school teacher on the island of Fehmarn. She was (and is, as we shall see) a tough lady. She was charmed by the tall young officer who came to woo her with his violin tucked under his arm. More than four decades later she still maintained, 'I would never have married him if he hadn't played the violin so beautifully.'* *

---

* Many years later he was to repeat the performance at another venue. Sent to Switzerland as Germany's Interpol representative, he was angered that the Swiss were not flying the swastika. . . . During the night he shinned up the side of the hotel building in total darkness and hoisted the flag. Next morning the Swiss were shocked to find the German banner flying above their hotel.
* * In German: '*Ich haette ihn . . . nicht geheiratet, haette er nicht so schoen Geige gespielt*'. Unfortunately the German verb '*geigen*' (to play the violin) has a double meaning. In German slang it means 'to fuck'.

7

But, though now engaged, he still continued his pursuit of women. Unfortunately, one of his conquests was the daughter of an important naval engineer, closely associated with stuffy Admiral Raeder, head of the German Navy. When the tearful 'daughter from a good house' told her father that Reinhard was engaged to be married the indignant parent reported the matter to Raeder and the fat was in the fire.

The Court of Honour, made up of four admirals, weren't impressed by Heydrich's excuses or his attitude. Time and again during the preceedings he said scornfully that it didn't matter to him one bit what an officer of the German Navy was *supposed* to do. *He* did what he wanted.

The result was predictable. He was dismissed from the *Kriegsmarine* for 'conduct unbecoming a naval officer' with a bridging, monthly payment of two hundred Reichsmark for two years. It was April, 1931, and *Oberleutnant zur See* Heydrich found himself on the scrap heap at a time when the Weimar Republic was evidently failing and six million Germans were out of work. His dream of one day becoming an admiral was over and, in addition, he now had a wife to support.

What was he to do? His seventy-year-old father was struggling to keep his head above water in Halle. His brother Heinz had given up his university studies and was earning a pittance as a casual labourer. Obviously there was nothing for him in his home town. He considered for a while that he might have a future as a mate in the Merchant Marine, but he changed his mind when his wife suggested a way of getting back into uniform. He should apply for a full-time job with Heinrich Himmler's SS. Heydrich jumped at the idea. For, like so many Germans of his class and time, he dearly loved a uniform. Somehow he found the train fare to Munich and set off on the journey which would change his whole life.

Himmler got down to business immediately. The sallow-faced pedant with his schoolmaster's pince-nez asked what he had been in the Navy and Heydrich told him he had been a *Nachrichtenoffizier* (in his case a signals officer). That interested Himmler, for he took the German word, which has both meanings, as 'intelligence officer'. He told Heydrich he wanted to build up an intelligence service for the SS and was currently looking for someone to run the organization. 'If you think you can do it,' Himmler continued 'go away for twenty minutes and sketch out a scheme for an intelligence department. Show me how you would do it.'

Heydrich got the point immediately. The SS didn't need a signals department; that was obvious. He went away and racked his brain. He had received a few hours' training in the Navy on intelligence matters, but he had long been an avid reader of spy novels dealing with the legendary British Secret Service. Eagerly he set to work.

Half an hour later his plan of organization, well loaded with military jargon remembered from his days in the *Kriegsmarine*, was finished and Himmler accepted him into the SS. A few days after that he joined the Hamburg branch of the full-time SS as a simple *Sturmann*, equivalent to an ordinary private. For a month or two thereafter, as Himmler described it in Heydrich's death eulogy in 1942, 'He stayed in Hamburg, side by side with out-of-work lads, taking part in the beer cellar brawls in the red light areas of that city. Then I called him to Munich and gave him a job in the as yet small leadership group at the Party HQ.'

Heydrich seized the opportunity with both hands. It was the start of a career behind the scenes which would shake Europe for the next decade. One day the failed naval officer would show the big shots of the Navy what he could do. As he put it to an assembly of Gestapo and security police officers in 1939, with Admiral Canaris, the mysterious head of the German Secret Service, sitting at his side, 'You see me before you, gentlemen, the one-time humble little First Lieutenant of the *Kriegsmarine*, sitting here with Admiral Canaris!'

Such was the young officer who faced the three police officials that August evening in 1939. Looking at him, with his long intelligent face and small foxlike eyes, Naujocks said many years later, 'I felt an ice-cold shudder run down my spine.' The feeling was justified.

9

3

For a while Heydrich paced back and forth, as if he were alone, taking absolutely no notice of the other three officers. Then he stopped, turned and stared around at them, almost as if he were surprised to find them there. 'Gentlemen,' he said, 'I have asked you to come here to discuss the execution of an order which has come from the Führer himself. We are concerned with a matter which goes far beyond anything we have ever done before.' Then he got down to business. 'We are concerned with a mission which will attract worldwide attention. For it, we will need two hundred men. That means there will be two hundred people in the know.' He lowered his voice at the words and turned his gaze on Naujocks. The 'intellectual gangster' shuddered. He knew that Heydrich wouldn't hesitate to get rid of him, or anyone else, if he stood in the way of his plans. After all, the Führer himself had called him 'the man with the iron heart'. There was a pause while Heydrich let his words about the 'two hundred people' who would be 'in the know' sink in. They knew instinctively what those words signified – two hundred people who subsequently would have to be got rid of.

But Heydrich didn't dwell on that problem. Instead he turned to Müller and snapped, 'You will provide at least fifty people from the concentration camps.' Müller nodded. Heydrich had brought him to Berlin despite objections from the Party faithful whom Müller had 'persecuted' in the old days before Hitler had taken over in 1933. He knew that Heydrich would expect him to find the fifty 'bodies' at Dachau Concentration Camp just north of the Bavarian capital. Then Heydrich confirmed his thinking. He said, 'As only dead people can keep their traps shut. . . .' He didn't finish the sentence. Instead he snapped, '*Sie verstehen*?' Müller certainly did understand. '*Jawohl, Gruppenführer,*' he growled and clicked his heels together under the little occasional table in the *Sitzecke**.

'What about the others?' Naujocks asked.

'I'll pick them. The best men available. Real men who are scared of nothing. *Klar*?'

Naujocks thought for a moment. Müller would pick fifty victims who would be 'liquidated'. Heydrich would pick the rest. Obviously this was going to be a big operation. Though he didn't yet know what it was, still he asked, 'How are we going to keep the operation secret?'

Instead of answering Naujocks' question, Heydrich posed one of his own: 'What would *you* do?'

Naujocks was caught off guard. He said hesitantly, 'Subject them to a special oath.' But even as he said the words he knew they were foolish. Only dead men couldn't talk. So would Heydrich kill the men he himself had picked? Naujocks shuddered. He too was one of those soon to be in the know.

Heydrich shook his head. 'We can't take that risk. But, nobody, is going to harm them. Afterwards they will be given plenty of opportunity to sacrifice themselves for Folk, Fatherland and Führer'. Mockingly, he used the standard formula of the time. 'They will be allowed to die a soldier's death at the front.'

He stared at them as if waiting for them to make some objection. Finally Naujocks broke the silence: 'At the front?' Front meant war!

Heydrich nodded. 'Yes, at the front. There is going to be a war and we, gentlemen, are going to start it – he paused – 'with the men we will select tomorrow morning.'

* Literally 'sitting corner', a small table and a couple of easy chairs.

On Thursday, 22 August, 1939, three weeks after that little conference in the Prinze Albrechtstrasse in Berlin, Hitler summoned his top generals to a secret conference at his chalet in the Bavarian Alps above the town of Berchtesgaden.

In the years he had spent on 'The Mountain', as it was called by the Party bigshots, he had hosted many conferences there, often of great importance. In 1937 he had fooled the Duke of Windsor into believing that, under certain circumstances, he might return to the throne of Britain. A year later he had duped Chamberlain, the British Prime Minister, letting him fly home to wave that 'scrap of paper' which would ensure 'peace in our time'. Here, too, Czechoslovakia had been carved up and the 'scrap of paper' shown to be worthless.

But never had the *Berghof* seen a conference of such importance as this one. Omitting his usual opening harangue, Hitler told the top brass straight out that the *Wehrmacht* was about to attack Poland, which stood alone since he had signed a secret pact with Stalin in which Russia agreed to remain neutral in any future conflict. (In reality the two dictators were to split Poland between them.) As for the Western Allies, Hitler had taken the measure of them during the 'Munich Crisis' of the previous year. They had indeed stood security for Poland's neutrality, but he had good reason to believe that neither France nor Britain would lift a finger to help Poland when the crunch came.

Now he launched himself into a long harangue after all – he loved the sound of his own voice – breaking off at intervals to raise his right leg and fart; due to his diet and the sixty pills a day prescribed by the various quacks who treated him, he broke wind all the time, even in the presence of women.

For hours he ranted at them, his eyes bulging, his sallow face turning red as he worked himself into one of his artificial rages. He screamed at them, 'Close your hearts to pity! Act brutally! Eighty million people, [the Germans] *must* have what is their right!'

Suddenly his rage vanished and he seemed perfectly calm. Now quite in control of himself, he told them that he would give them the date for the planned attack on Poland the next day. There was no question of backing down now. All he needed was a justification for the war, which would look good to the German people and to the neutral powers. It was *real-politik* of the worst kind. 'I shall give a propaganda reason for starting the war whether it's plausible or not. The victor will not be asked afterwards if he told the truth. In starting and waging a war it is not right that matters, but victory.'

None of them knew that Heydrich had been working on the 'propaganda reason' since the first of the month. At the earlier meeting at Gestapo HQ he had told Naujocks, 'You, as my special agent, will have a specially dangerous mission. You will lead the attack on the German frontier radio station at Gleiwitz, just inside the German border with Poland, with a handful of men dressed as Polish civilians. You will force your way into the station and capture it. One of your men, a Polish speaker, will harangue Germany over the air in Polish, so it will appear that the Poles have captured the place. As Gleiwitz is linked to the main German radio network, most of Germany will hear his words. They will also hear the cries of the wounded and the German station employees shouting for help.'

That had been in the first week of August. Now, as Josef Goebbels, the Minister of Propaganda and Public Enlightenment, stepped up his newspaper hate campaign against the Poles, 'Operation Himmler' as it was code-named, moved relentlessly forward.

Heydrich had agents posted around the area of operations so that the ordinary *Wehrmacht* units in the district, who had not been put in the picture, would not move in when the shooting started. Admiral Canaris, head of the Secret Service, had been roped in to provide Polish uniforms, while Müller had found the 'canned goods' (the concentration camp inmates) who would be found dead at the scene of the 'Incident' in due course. Because Heydrich wanted neutral journalists to be flown into the Gleiwitz area once the attack was over so that they could see the blood, the unfortunate victims would first be given a lethal injection and shot when they were dead – macabre but important. Detail after detail was added with German thoroughness.

While outside his own little world events moved fast on the stage of Central Europe, Naujocks took up his post in the Hotel

Oberschlesischen Hof in Gleiwitz, while his agents stayed in other hotels and lodging houses, avoiding each other in public. If they chanced to meet in the street, they looked the other way. They looked no different from the locals, except, perhaps that they were bigger and stronger. Their clothes were Polish-made and bore tailors' marks from Lodz or other Polish cities and were mostly the product of Jewish sweated labour. Their pockets were filled with tram tickets, cigarette packets and other items of Polish origin. Their wallets bulged with Polish *zloty*. 'Everything conceivable had been taken care of,' Naujocks said when he spoke of the Gleiwitz Incident at the Nuremberg Trials.

But all the same he was uneasy. His mind kept returning to the last words that Heydrich had said to him at that Berlin meeting: 'One more thing, Naujocks. If the alarm should be sounded before you can complete the operation or if the police should be called in before you can get away, I don't want to see you alive again. The only favour you can do me then is to ensure that your body cannot be identified.' As he said afterwards, 'Obviously Heydrich saw in me one of those few in the know who had to be destroyed. I'd already done too much of his dirty work for him and this was a particularly suitable opportunity to get rid of me for good.'

4

In Berlin the propaganda war against Poland mounted. The Goebbels-controlled papers – which really meant all of them – pulled out all the stops. The Berlin *BZ*, for instance, headlined on 26 August: 'COMPLETE CHAOS IN POLAND – GERMAN FAMILIES FLEE – POLISH SOLDIERS PUSH TO EDGE OF GERMAN BORDER.' The *I2 Uhr Blatt* reported, under banner headlines: 'THIS PLAYING WITH FIRE HAS GONE TOO FAR . . . THREE GERMAN PASSENGER PLANES SHOT AT BY POLES . . . IN CORRIDOR MANY GERMAN FARM-HOUSES IN FLAMES*.' Hitler's own paper, the *Völkischer Beobachter* summed it up in inch-high headlines: 'WHOLE OF POLAND IN WAR FEVER. 1,500,000 MEN MOBILIZED. UNINTER-RUPTED TROOP TRANSPORT TOWARD THE FRONTIER. CHAOS IN UPPER SILESIA.'

If there was chaos in Polish Upper Silesia Naujocks knew nothing of it. He spent his days inspecting the Gleiwitz Radio Station and the surrounding area. The station itself was situ-ated outside the town on a secondary road leading to the smaller town of Tarnowitz and was surrounded by a two-metre-high fence. Otherwise the radio station, consisting of the small studio and two blocks of living quarters, was practically unguarded, save for its middle-aged watchmen.

All the same, knowing that his life was on the line, Naujocks took the greatest of care in reconnoitring the place. Minutely he surveyed the entrance. He judged the height of the various

* The 'Polish corridor' between Germany and its province, East Prussia.

15

storeys. He assessed the inner distance between the exit and the fence. In particular he considered all the possible escape routes. As he said later, 'My life depended upon them. I didn't want to be one of the dead shown to the world press on the day after the raid to prove that "Polish insurgents" had started the war.'

On 25 August the collection of wooden huts which housed the miserable, pyjama-clad* inmates of Sachsenhausen Concentration Camp was placed under *'Barrackensperre'* (literally 'confined to huts'). There would be no work that day, but the news didn't make the inmates particularly happy. They were all Germans and they had heard enough during the last few days to know that something fishy was going on. Why had they received repeated visits from high-ranking SS officers? Why had four prisoners, the Hamburger Ludwig W., Harry von B., Walter Sch. from Wuppertal and Wilhelm B. from Straussberg, just outside Berlin, been specially inspected?

Around midday that Friday the inmates' suspicions were confirmed. Four black cars drove up to the cell block at high speed and a few minutes later the four prisoners were brought out heavily chained, and put into the cars. The next day others were taken away, never to return – save one. He was Ludwig W. After the war he reported: 'I was taken in chains to Berlin by two civilian warders. From there I travelled in a closed compartment to Breslau where I was placed in solitary confinement in a local jail. After two days he was told that there had been a mistake and he was being sent back to Sachsenhausen. There he was confined in a blacked-out cell, again in solitary, until 11 May, 1940. He had been very lucky, for he was the sole survivor of *Aktion Konserve*, Gestapo Müller's cruelly named 'Operation Canned Goods'.

A few days later Müller, who had set up a temporary headquarters at Oppeln not far from Gleiwitz, explained to Naujocks how he intended to use the Canned Goods: He said

---

* The pyjamas were modelled on ones worn by US prisoners in the 19th century.

that he had picked a dozen or so criminals, who had already been sentenced for their crimes. They would be dressed in Polish uniforms and their bodies would be left at the scene of the Gleiwitz attack. It would thus appear that they had been killed during the attack. Heydrich had personally selected a doctor who would give them a lethal injection before they were shot. The men heavily drugged, would be taken to Gleiwitz where they would be shot' their bodies turned this way and that before they received the fatal bullet so that it would appear they had been shot from the front by the defenders of the radio station.

That evening Naujocks went out for a quick beer. When he returned to the Ober-Schlesischen Hof the porter told him that there was a gentleman on the phone from Berlin asking for him urgently. He knew who that 'gentleman from Berlin' was all right. It was Heydrich. He told Naujocks not to leave his hotel room from now onwards under any circumstances. The machinery had been set in motion and there could be no turning back. Naujocks must expect the code signal for the operation at any moment. It was to be *'Grossmutter gestorben'* (Grandmother dead). Then he must act immediately – and with that the line went dead.

The actors were in place, the scene was set, the play could begin.

Thursday, 31 August, 1939, the last day of peace in Europe, was hot and sticky in the Polish-German border area. Naujocks looked out of the window of his hotel room, where he had been waiting for four days now, at the handful of men and women in the dusty street below. The men were in their shirt sleeves, their jackets carried over their arms; the women were in damp floral frocks. How unconcerned they all looked! They went about their business as if things were always going to go on like this. Naujocks knew differently. Four hours before, just as he had been going down for lunch, the porter had handed him a telegram. It was from Berlin and he knew what it contained. He opened it and read the two words that signified the start of the Second World War.

Now the wheels began to turn with ever-increasing speed.

17

From nearby Oppeln the trucks carrying Müller's canned goods were already rolling. Picked units of the SS had taken up their positions in the district, sealing it off, even from the *Wehrmacht*, poised for the invasion of Poland. All local civilian police posts were under surveillance. Heydrich didn't want them blundering into the picture. By now Naujocks had contacted his agents. They had been told to be ready for action at a quarter to eight that night.

The sun was setting when he and his men took up their positions in the vicinity of the radio station. Nervously they puffed at their cheap Polish cigarettes – even that had been taken into consideration. Indeed, later, when the investigators did their work, they found the incriminating Polish cigarette ends. They were a scruffy-looking bunch in their cheap working clothes provided by Canaris's *Abwehr*. But they were all eager Nazis, haters of the *Polacken*, champing at the bit as they waited to go into action.

'Three men will wait here,' Naujocks snapped. 'If anyone comes along, give the alarm. If anyone tries to enter the building after us, shoot him at once.'

He jerked his head in the direction of the radio building, 'Let's go.'

As casually as they could, the men started to walk down the road to the compound. They reached the gate. Now they were only fifty metres off the entrance to the radio building itself.

The night porter was an old man with sunken cheeks and a straggling moustache. One of them stuck his big pistol under the porter's nose. 'Hands up,' he cried in rough Polish. And if the porter didn't understand the words, he understood the gesture well enough. His hands flew into the air.

Naujocks and his five companions ran on up the steps. An engineer named Foitzek spotted them and opened his mouth to protest, but no words came when he saw the muzzle of a pistol pointing at his stomach. Naujocks pushed past him to be confronted by the radio station's staff. He didn't give them time to collect themselves 'Hands up!' he yelled and jerked up his pistol muzzle to indicate what they were supposed to do. Then he pushed them aside.

Telling his story later, Naujocks explained, 'We then fired our pistols in the broadcasting room. We loosed off a couple of shots into the ceiling in order to frighten the people and make a bit of a shindig.'

The radio staff were soon handcuffed, but then Naujocks hit an unexpected problem. He didn't know how to broadcast! As he admitted later, 'We had a feverish search before we could get our broadcast through.' Frantically, knowing that time was running out, he and his men checked the unfamiliar array of dials and knobs until they came across something called the 'storm microphone'. This was normally used to inform local listeners that the quality of a broadcast might be interfered with by some storm in the area. Naujocks pulled out the prepared harangue in Polish and handed it to one of his men who spoke Polish. Most of them were what the Germans called *Wasserpolacken* – water Poles, ie half-German. The man grabbed it and, to the accompaniment of staged shots and excited German voices, he gabbled off the message. It lasted exactly four minutes. Then it was time to go. They clattered down the stairs and out into the open. Dramatically draped across the entrance was one of Müller's 'canned goods'. Two of the three men posted outside had collected him from the Gestapo truck and put him there. Naujocks gave him a fleeting glance. The gunshot wound looked realistic enough – as if he had been killed while rushing up the stairs. Naujocks gave the pre-arranged signal and the SS men ran towards the waiting truck.

5

Next morning Hitler's own paper, the *Völkischer Beobachter*, bore the banner headline: 'POLISH INSURGENTS CROSS THE GERMAN FRONTIER'. The editorial went on to explain that the 'Gleiwitz crime' was clearly the signal 'for a general attack on German territory by Polish guerrillas'. A few hours later Hitler summoned the Party's *Reichstag*, the rubber-stamp German Parliament. They listened as he thundered from the rostrum, his face rouged and made up, as crazy as ever, that 'since four forty-five this morning our cannon have been firing back!' The Third Reich was at war with Poland. The tragedy had begun.

Meanwhile the world's press had rushed to the scene of the crime – 'that dastardly Polish provocation', as the Germans called it. Here Müller appeared, investigating the 'incident', lecturing the attentive correspondents with the help of a detailed model of the radio station, accurate in every way (which it should have been; it had been made weeks before for Heydrich's men to train with), while in the background the mastermind behind the plan, Heydrich, nodded his head gravely, muttering at intervals, 'Yes, yes, that's how the war started.'

That afternoon of Friday, 1st September, 1939, while Heydrich and his black-clad cronies celebrated the success of their first major mission of the Second World War, his one-time chief from his days in the German Navy, and now his rival in the shadow war, Admiral Canaris, was in a mood of deep depression. He was a strange man, whom nobody seemed to be able to assess correctly, then or now. It was said that he always felt cold and it is certainly true that he wore a greatcoat even in the height of summer. He had a wife and two daughters, but seemed more attached to his two dachshunds and his North African servant than he did to them. He hated the sight of military uniform and when he had to wear one he did so reluctantly and in a very sloppy manner. One of his few pleasures was to put on an apron and cook four-course meals for his agents.

Yet he was a ruthless spymaster who was said to have been the lover of the famed female spy, Mata Hari, of First World War One fame and whom he had betrayed to the French when she became too dangerous for him. It was said he had escaped from British imprisonment by killing the Italian priest who had come to hear his confession and donning his cassock. He had also been involved in the deaths of the German communist revolutionaries Rosa Luxemburg and Karl Liebknecht.

On this day when Heydrich was celebrating the success of his operation Canaris was at his own HQ at Berlin's Tirpitzstrasse sending orders out to his agents throughout the world now that the war had at last begun. In the dimly lit room – he had a phobia about wasting money and was always turning out lights – he said to one of his subordinates, 'This means the end of Germany.'

II

WAR IN THE SHADOWS

'My experience is that the gentlemen who
are the best behaved and the most sleek
are those who are doing the mischief. We
cannot be too sure of anybody.'

Lord Ironside, C-in-C Home Forces,
addressing Home Guard volunteers,
England, June, 1940.

1

At a quarter to nine on the night of 8 November, 1939, two customs men stood in the darkness of a garden on the German side of Lake Constance. They were listening to the Führer's annual broadcast from Munich which was coming to them through the open window of the local reformatory. This by now traditional speech he always delivered from the beer cellar which had been the Party's main haunt before he came to power.

At first they didn't notice the undersized figure ten or twelve metres away in the dark. But when they did see him, he appeared, like themselves, to be engrossed in the Führer's speech. Probably he was a harmless civilian and a patriotic German, but he *was* only a hundred metres from the border which they were paid to guard.

One of them cried, '*Hallo, sie da was machen Sie, ja?*' and, without waiting for a reply, he unslung his rifle and walked towards the man, who quickly raised his hands.

Minutes later he was standing in the yellow light cast by the unshaded bulb in the customs post at the Kreuzlinger Tor. His pockets were emptied and his belongings spread out on the table in front of the somewhat puzzled officials. His identity card showed that he was one Georg Elser, a carpenter by trade. Also in his possession were a bundle of leaflets, a postcard of the Munich *Burgerbraukeller*, where the Führer was still making his speech, and a few pieces of metal which one of the customs men who had served in the army identified as parts of a time-detonator.

'A time detonator?' the sergeant in charge exclaimed in surprise. 'What the devil would he be doing with a detonator?'

'Don't ask me, Sarge,' answered the former soldier with evident lack of interest.

It was just about that time–twenty minutes past nine o'clock, half an hour after the obscure little carpenter had been arrested – that the *Burgerbraukeller* was shattered by a violent explosion. The pillar behind the podium at which the Führer had been speaking simply disappeared. A moment later the roof started to cave in, covering the screaming crowd below with plaster.

Six of Hitler's 'Old Fighters', as the men who had supported him before his take-over in 1933 were called, were killed outright, as well as one of the waitresses. Sixty-three men and women were injured, sixteen of them seriously. But the man for whom that bomb had been intended had left thirteen minutes earlier. Due to the war situation he had cut his traditional speech and so escaped one more of the many attempts on his life.

The alarm signals sounded throughout Germany. Heydrich, Himmler and Müller all prepared to take over. A state of emergency was proclaimed and the order went out to seal off the frontiers. No one must leave Germany until the instigator of this dastardly attack had been apprehended. By midnight the order had reached the sergeant in charge of the Kreuzlinger Tor post. He remembered the carpenter's postcard of the beer cellar and the bits of the time detonator. Even his sluggish mind must have realized that perhaps he had caught the big fish.

Georg Elser, though a good carpenter, was perhaps not altogether right in the head. A former communist, he was possessed of an *idée fixe*. He had to save the working classes from the horrors of another world war, and the only way he could do that, he believed, was by getting rid of Hitler.

Amazingly enough, throughout the war powerful Germans with all kinds of resources at their disposal tried to do the same, but none came as close as Elser to succeeding. As soon as the war began he had set to work. He gave up his job and started stealing high explosive from a quarry where he had once worked. Then, knowing that Hitler spoke each year in Munich on 9 November, and with a plan already beginning to form in his slightly muddled mind, he moved to the Bavarian capital. Each night he broke into the Burgerbraukeller, hiding himself in the cloakroom until all the guests and the staff had gone. Then he burrowed into the big pillar behind the rostrum from which Hitler would speak. There, after weeks of work, he deposited a time bomb, sealed up the hole and left, firmly convinced, as he later told the Gestapo, 'that in this way I could get rid of the leadership'.

Hitler never rid himself of the suspicion that this could not be the work of one man, especially that of a simple German worker. Even as Nuremberg Police Chief Martin stopped the 'Führer Special' that night to tell Hitler of the news from Munich, the thought flashed through his mind that this *had* to be the work of the British Secret Service. He was particularly suspicious of the only real British SIS outpost left on the Continent, the one in Holland, using mainly German exiles and run by two military men of the old school, Captain Payne Best and Major Stevens.

Working from the usual cover of Passport Control Officer at the British Legation in The Hague, the British had been building up a network of agents in the Reich ever since Hitler had come to power. When the British agents in Germany, who included naval architects, nuns and even a former champion cycle racer, started to be troublesome, Heydrich began to look at the network more closely.

As his Trojan Horse he had used agent F479, a German émigré whose real name was Dr Franz and who, as the Germans say, had been 'kissed on both cheeks', ie, a double agent. Through Franz, Heydrich fed Captain Best half-truths about the strength of the German Army's supposed resistance to Hitler. In return he discovered the degree of co-operation between the British and Dutch Intelligence services and information regarding British feelings about Germany's desire for war. Because of the importance of this latter information and the persistent desire of the British establishment to

27

appease Germany, Himmler, who was Heydrich's superior, had personally informed the Führer about this 'war in the shadows' being waged in Holland.

Now, as Hitler raved about the 'machinations of the British Secret Service', Himmler decided to do something. He ordered that contact with the two British Secret Service chiefs in Holland should be increased. He needed to know at once about their role, if any, in the Elser murder attempt and so, in the early hours of the very next morning, he called the SD officer directly responsible for conducting the Dutch operation at his HQ in Düsseldorf.

Walter Schellenberg was another of Heydrich's 'intellectual gangsters', only much smarter than Naujocks.

'Listen carefully,' Himmler said. 'Do you know what has happened?' Schellenberg replied in the negative.

'Last night, just after the Führer's speech in the beer cellar, an attempt was made to assassinate him. A bomb went off. Luckily he'd left the cellar a few minutes before. But there is no doubt that the British Secret Service is behind it. The Führer and I were already on the train to Berlin when we got the news. He says – and this is an order – that when you meet the agents tomorrow you are to arrest them and bring them to Germany. This may mean a violation of Dutch territory, but the Führer says that is of no consequence. The SS detachment that's already been assigned to protect you is to help you carry out your mission. Do you understand?'

'Yes, *Reichsführer*, but . . .'

'There are no buts, ' Himmler cut him short sharply. 'Do you understand?'

Lamely Schellenberg answered, '*Jawohl.*'

Thus Schellenberg, for the first time since he had joined Heydrich's SD, was faced with real danger. In those years he had been instrumental in building up the secret service side of Heydrich's police *apparat*. Often he had worked seventeen hours a day, only allowing himself an hour off in the morning to go riding and a short time in the evening to gloat over his collection of pornographic photos. Now he knew he must carry out Himmler's order whatever the danger.

It was almost a month since he had first met the two British agents, both retired Army officers with Intelligence experience gained in India. They looked foppish, especially the one with the monocle, but Schellenberg knew they both carried automatics and wouldn't hesitate to use them if necessary.

At the first meeting he had used the cover of *Hauptmann* Schemmel of the *Wehrmacht*'s transport department. Equipped with some carefully doctored military 'secrets', he had convinced the two middle-aged British agents that he was genuine and that he represented a senior group among Hitler's generals who wished to overthrow the Führer with Britain's help.

There had been a slight hiccup during that meeting. When the group crossed the border the Dutch had searched his luggage, presumably on British orders. During the search a bottle of aspirins had tumbled out on to the desk. To his horror Schellenberg noticed that they were marked '*SS Sanitätshauptamt*' (SS Main Medical Office) and quickly knocked the tablets on to the floor. A little while later he thought he had been rumbled once more when Captain Best caught him unawares in the bathroom and asked him, 'Do you always wear a monocle?' Schellenberg countered the query with, 'You know, I've been meaning to ask you the same question' and with that the awkward moment passed.

Now he felt that the British trusted him. They had even supplied him with one of their own radio transmitters so he could communicate with them directly each day. They had also given him a special Dutch Intelligence pass which allowed him to cross the frontier without hindrance. In other words, Schellenberg felt that he would be able to lure the two British agents and their Dutch helper across the frontier into the Reich without difficulty, just as Himmler had envisaged.

He guessed, however, that trouble would start as soon as they realized they were being 'arrested', as Himmler put it ('kidnapped' would have been a better description in Schellenberg's opinion). Obviously they would try and defend themselves. After all, they were agents, and armed, well aware

29

of what their fate would be if they fell into the hands of the Gestapo. Once the shooting started anything could happen. But he, at least, was going to be careful.

Stevens and Best sensed that something was wrong as soon as they neared the frontier post at the Dutch border town of Venlo. But they, too, knew that they had to go ahead with the meeting. For it seemed that their mission had come to the notice of the Prime Minister, Neville Chamberlain. For reasons that are obscure even to this day, he wanted to go ahead with negotiations with these 'representatives' of the 'German generals'. He was even prepared to risk his last major spy ring in Continental Europe to do so.

By now Britain had been at war with Germany for two months. Poland had fallen and the Western Allies had not raised a finger. Britain and France were still 'fighting' the 'phoney war' and the only casualty incurred by the Allies had been a French soldier who had been shot dead by a British sentry when he had not replied to the latter's challenge. Later it was discovered that the unfortunate *poilu* had been very deaf.

Critical voices were already asking when was Britain going to move. When was the British Army, poised since early September on the German frontier, going to attack? Apart from the Navy, commanded now by pugnacious, one-time political exile Winston Churchill, neither of the other two components of the British Armed Forces had taken any decisive action. What was really going on behind the scenes in London?

It seems that the British Government, still dominated by the appeasers, was using these meetings between the SIS and the 'representatives' of the dissident generals to try and work out the following deal. If the *Wehrmacht* could depose Hitler and replace him, *even* with another Nazi, say Goering who was acceptable to Whitehall, then both sides would conclude a peace. There would be no war. In return Germany would be left with its gains in Central Europe: Austria, Czechoslovakia and Poland. Who in the West cared about such places? Chamberlain had made that quite clear at the time of Munich. Now, in 1939, he had gone to war out of injured pride and personal prestige. After all, Hitler *had* tricked him at Munich with his 'peace in our time'.*

Now, their hand forced by an obscure, perhaps half-barmy, German carpenter, these people who might well have sealed the fate of Central Europe in 1939 if their discussions had been allowed to continue in their original form had been abruptly shoved into the war in the shadows. Not only that; by giving his authorization to this lethal little game, and what was to follow, the newly created *General der Polizei*** Reinhard Heydrich had unwittingly signed his own fate.***

* The last time the author asked when the relevant documents to what became known as the 'Venlo Incident' would be released to the general public, he was told *2015!* The date is indicative that the meeting between Schellenberg and the two British spymasters was much more important than was revealed at the time.
** Hitler had just awarded him this exalted rank at the age of 35 on account of the success of the 'Gleiwitz Incident'.
*** The three surviving main actors in this deadly little game, Stevens, Best and Schellenberg, were all blackmailed by the SIS by various means into not giving a true account of the background to the Venlo Incident.

2

The Germans were in position first. Three metres from the red-and-white-striped border crossing Schellenberg waited in the place's one café-cum-grocery store. He wasn't at ease, not only on account of the task in front of him and the hidden SD men, but also because of the 'mood' at the Venlo crossing. There seemed to be a lot of strangers about, accompanied by savage-looking Alsatian dogs. The Dutch frontier guards seemed unusually vigilant too. Normally they went about the routine of their everyday duties in a slow, bored manner. Today they were quick and alert. They kept their rifles slung, as if ready at a moment's notice to unsling them. As Schellenberg said later, 'Obviously our British friends had taken unusually thorough measures in preparation for this meeting.'

The wait in the dreary Café Backus dragged on. The sky over the flat grey Dutch plain grew darker. Schellenberg thought it would start to drizzle again soon. It always seemed to in Holland. He had grown to hate that cold thin Dutch rain over these last few weeks while he had been 'playing in the Heydrich theatre', as he described the affair later.

Every few minutes he caught himself looking at his wrist-watch. The British were late. Had they been warned? They had agents everywhere in the border area. The Dutch would work for anybody – for money.

He glanced at the customs post where Naujocks' big open car was waiting behind a wall. Nothing moved. He whispered a fervent prayer that the men of the 'snatch squad' had not been lulled into a false sense of security by the lack of action. Everything depended upon the speed with which they accomplished their mission before the Dutch were alerted.

Suddenly he heard a car approaching at speed. He sprang to his feet. His companion, de Crinis, a friend of the Heydrich family, pushed him down again. 'That's not the car,' he hissed. 'Relax.'

Best and Stevens, and their aide from the Dutch General Staff, Lieutenant Klop, using the cover name of Coppens, were just as uneasy. Dutch troops were everywhere in the border area. Something was in the air and they were relieved when a Dutch sentry stopped their car and told them they could go no further. Unfortunately, in the light of what was to come, Klop sorted out the problem and they were able to proceed.

Best, who was driving his big American Buick, did as he was commanded. They passed a second check point. Now they were driving along one of those typical dead-straight cobbled Dutch roads, fringed on both sides by trees. As Best recalled after the war, 'Somehow or other it seemed different from previous days. Then I noticed the German barrier. Up to now it had always been closed. Now it was open. There seemed nothing between us and the enemy.' He was right. There wasn't.

They came closer to the frontier. It all seemed peaceful enough. No one was in sight except a plump customs officer leaning against a wall and a little girl playing with a ball outside the café. Best slowed down. Klop said, 'Go ahead. Everything is all right.'

It was exactly three o'clock. Schellenberg had just ordered a coffee. He was about to take a sip when he heard the noise of the car. He put the cup down and rushed into the street, waving his hands as if the general from the German High Command, whom Best and Stevens were expecting, was inside the café.

Best stopped the car and they started to get out. At that moment a big open car roared out from behind the customs post. With the engine going full out, it seemed to fill the narrow street. Best caught a fleeting glimpse of what he later described as 'rough-looking men'. Two of them, standing on the car's running boards, were letting rip with machine pistols.

Klop reacted first. He threw himself out of the Buick and, drawing his service revolver, he began returning the fire. Schellenberg ducked. The slugs all seemed to be coming his way. Now Klop fired four accurate shots at the German Mercedes and the windscreen shattered. Schellenberg noticed how the 'crystalline threads were spreading from the bullet holes'.

Naujocks took on Klop. He sprang out of the flying car, ripped up his pistol and a regular duel between the two men began. Both shot deliberately, as if they were back on the range, taking careful aim. The Dutchman was hit and his pistol dropped from his fingers. His knees began to buckle beneath him. Slowly he fell to the ground in a pool of his own blood.

The main opponent taken care of, Naujocks, yelled at Schellenberg, whom he didn't like, 'Will you get the hell out of this. God knows why you haven't been hit. *Los.*'

Schellenberg needed no urging. He fled.

Meanwhile Best and Stevens had been seized. After years of easy living, it must have come as a great shock to the middle-aged officers to find themselves suddenly in the rough hands of the SD thugs. In the years to come (they were finally released in 1945 and returned to Britain in disgrace, threatened with the loss of their pensions if they ever told the real story behind the 'Venlo Incident') they must have had ample time to reflect upon that moment which so dramatically changed their lives. But they surrendered quietly enough, Stevens stretching out his hands to be handcuffed and mumbling to his companion, 'Our number's up, Best.'

It was. Now Naujocks' men urged them across into Germany. Moments later they were over the frontier. The operation had been a complete success and the two Englishmen were in the hands of Heydrich's dreaded police. The Germans could do with them as they wished.

This was Naujocks' last major field operation. Soon he would carry out the greatest forgery operation in history, one that is still recorded in the *Guinness Book of Records*. But in a way his involvement with what today would be called 'economic warfare' would be his undoing. He was accused by Heydrich of being party to an illegal gold transaction,* stripped of his rank and sent in due course to the Eastern Front as a private in an SS Penal Battalion. Surprisingly enough he survived and lasted another two years until he deserted to the British in Belgium in 1944. He ended his life as a one-eyed bouncer in a brothel-cum-bar in Hamburg's red-light district, the *Reeperbahn*.

Schellenberg came out of the 'Venlo Incident' with an Iron Cross, awarded personally by the Führer, but feeling that 'It would have been better if I could have continued the negotiations'. It is the only real slip that Schellenberg made in his memoirs, which were edited and doctored by his British SIS case officer after the war. It is obvious from that remark that Schellenberg knew that something more was going on at Venlo than simply talks between two hidebound SIS agents and the supposed representatives of the German 'military resistance'.

For a while, again according to Schellenberg, Himmler and Müller tried to get Elser to confess that he was in the pay of the British Secret Service. Once Schellenberg, meeting Müller, noticed that the latter was nursing bruised knuckles and he could guess why. Müller told him that 'Elser either refuses to say anything or tells stupid lies'. He added 'I've never had a man before me yet whom I didn't break in the end,' and Schellenberg believed him.

But Müller never did make Elser talk. He remained in the same concentration camp in Southern Germany as Best and Stevens, making wooden models with his old tools, which had been brought to him on Himmler's express order, until April, 1945, when he was 'killed in air raid'. In other words,

* Some say Heydrich wanted to be rid of him because Naujocks listened in to one of Heydrich's love-making sessions in the high-class 'Salon Kitty' brothel which Heydrich had opened in Berlin before the war for foreign diplomats and the like.

discreetly liquidated, presumably also on Himmler's orders. For by then Himmler was secretly negotiating behind Hitler's back with the Western Allies and didn't want memories from the past spoiling the talks.*

But if by the start of 1940 Stevens and Best had lost their initial value – from now on the British authorities were very chary about making contact with the German 'resistance' – their masters in Britain were still of interest to Heydrich. After those early triumphs at Gleiwitz and Venlo it seemed that nothing could check his progress. Already, at 35, he was a general and a secretary of state, though it irritated him that he could never report directly to the Führer in either of these capacities, but always had to go through Himmler; but that was not enough for him. Secretly he had taken up flying. Already he was a reserve major in the *Luftwaffe* and soon he would attempt his first operational sortie against the British. He crash-landed, was grounded and returned chastened to Berlin with both his hands heavily bandaged.

He had also extended his bureaucratic activities. Now he was well on his way to having a card-index on every living German over the age of 18. But even that wasn't enough. He trawled ancient police records of pimps, prostitutes and police informers to dig up any dirt he could find on his bosses and party comrades. Obviously he thought that blackmail was another way to gain power. For the same reason he had instituted the 'Salon Kitty', a fashionable brothel in Berlin, staffed by high-class whores, who allegedly also spoke several languages in which they pumped their illustrious clients and where all important pillow talk was recorded below in the cellars.

Thus, by the time the phoney war of 1939 was transformed into the hot one of the spring of 1940 Heydrich was in complete charge of the hearts and minds of eighty million Germans and an equal number of newly acquired Austrians, Czechoslovaks

* For a while Best and Stevens thought they'd suffer the same fate that spring of 1945, but they were spared, being used as hostages by the SS. But although they survived into the fifties, they were never allowed to tell the truth about the Venlo Incident.

and Poles in an Empire that would soon stretch from the bogs of the old Polish-Russian frontier to the English Channel.

He had become even more of a loner, telling his wife that she should limit her circle of acquaintances. When she protested that she was being neglected and that she rarely saw him, he replied, 'We've got each other. Let us enjoy ourselves in the privacy of our home with the children.' All the same he still allowed himself the odd drunken orgy, which usually ended in a brothel. Once, after a party in an Italian brothel, he drew a handful of gold coins from his pocket and threw them on the floor, enjoying the spectacle of the half-naked whores scrambling for them.

Indeed he seemed possessed by a kind of obsessive secrecy, as if he wished no one, even his wife, to know too much about his affairs or his plans. Once Himmler offered him the great honour of the informal 'thou'. Tactfully, Heydrich turned this down, although Himmler only used this intimate form of address with a few old Party comrades, including one of the most notorious spies of the Second World War Two, the celebrated Paul Thuemmel. Behind his back Heydrich continued to mock Himmler and his plain bourgeois wife with her 'size forty knickers'.

One could say that Heydrich was typical of that second generation of Nazis, who had arrived on the scene in the early thirties: men like Bormann, Speer, Peiper of the Waffen SS, even Schellenberg, who, starting as junior technocrats of power after Hitler had taken over in 1933, had acquired, over the years, a taste for it. Now, in their own devious ways, often working in the Party's backrooms, they were out to achieve control for themselves. They had realized that Hitler, Himmler, Goering and the rest wouldn't survive for ever. Who would succeed them? The answer was obviously – they themselves. But in order to do so, they had to acquire a record and, more importantly, a power basis, the platform which all politicians need if they are to make it to the top.

Now, as the war moved into its second year, Heydrich felt it was not enough to be second-in-command of Germany's police system, even though that made him one of the most powerful men in the Reich. The very nature of the post made it one hardly known to the general public. He had to play a more prominent role in what was regarded as politics by the Nazis. But what? How could he become more than a 'police blood-hound', as he often described himself in disgust to Lina?

In early 1940, as a kind of follow-up to what he had already learned through the 'Venlo Incident' of strange undercurrents at the very top of British politics, the opportunity came along in the shape of a British Prince of the Realm, who was more German than he himself.

3

The last of his illustrious ancestors to have English blood in his veins had been James I, three hundred years before his own birth in the last decade of the nineteenth century. Since then there had been generation after generation on the British throne who were purely German. For nearly two hundred years the Hanoverian rulers, his immediate ancestors, had married the offspring of the German principalities which had survived the dissolution of the Holy Roman Empire. Both his great-grandparents, Victoria and Albert, had spoken German before they ever learned English, while his grandfather, Edward VII, again married to a princess of a German royal family, spoke English with a decidedly German accent. In short the future Prince of Wales was of pure German descent and, although he spoke English in a 'kind of bastardized cockney-American', as one observer put it unkindly, the only foreign language which he spoke correctly and with the right accent was German.

Not that he particularly liked the Germans in the beginning. Just as he reacted against the blue-blooded pomp and ceremony of the British court, he scorned the provincial stuffiness of the German courts, where all the men wore Ruritanian uniforms, whether they were entitled to them or not, and there was constant bowing and scraping.

As a handsome, blond, somewhat undersized Guards officer, he had gone to France during the First World War, naturally on the staff, and had come to dislike the Germans even more, although he had more blood relatives fighting on the German than on the Allied side. By 1918 one could say that there existed a strange confused love-hate relationship between Edward, Prince of Wales, next in line to the British throne, and that Germany from which his distant and more immediate forefathers had come.

But then 'Eddie', as he was known to the family, dominated by a strict father who treated his sons as if they were able seamen in the Royal Navy, was an altogether confused person. Although he was popular and apparently very concerned about the lot of the common man, he was at heart an empty-headed playboy. He ignored protocol. He did his duty as the heir to the throne only when his father forced him to do so. His own pleasure was paramount.

In particular, his confused sex life dominated his behaviour and, in the end, his attitudes and political reasoning. In the first place he wasn't easy with adult sexual relationships. His mistresses were usually older, married women with children, who would tolerate his sexual whims, but on the whole ones who would dominate him. Behind his back one of them, his first long-time mistress, Freda Dudley-Ward, the wife of the head of the parliamentary liberal faction called him 'the little man' because, as another long-time mistress, the American Thelma Furness, confided to her friends, 'He has the smallest pecker I've ever seen on a man'.

Whether these hard-bitten society women replaced the loving mother he had never had or the nannies and nurses who had been his constant companions in his youth and had ruled him in his nursery is not important, but it is clear that his relationships always depended on his being dominated by a strong woman.

Within this same sexual framework, his idea of fun among friends was definitely infantile. His cousin Lord Louis Mountbatten reported how, on the cruise he took with 'Eddie' in 1920, he had himself dressed in a nappie and pushed around, complete with pacifier, in a pram. On the same cruise, dressed in drag, he launched himself at Lord Claud Hamilton, a handsome officer in the Grenadier Guards, and stripped him naked. No one questioned why he had done so.

40

After all, he was the heir to the throne.

Finally, as all the world knows, his sexual hang-ups landed him with that fatal last mistress, Wallis. She was neither pretty, intelligent nor British. But she *did* have enough cunning to give him what he wanted in and out of bed. In return he had to give the Southern Belle on the make what *she* wanted, and that was money, power, titles and social status.

In the year after his abdication the Duke of Windsor, as he had then become, went to see Adolf Hitler. Hitler looked forward to the meeting, though he normally had little time for royalty. But in the autumn of that year he went out of his way to spend two hours with the Duke and Duchess of Windsor at Berchtesgaden. He was particularly taken by Wallis – 'no make-up, not a bad figure and impeccable grooming and couture'. It was the start of a strange relationship between the descendant of Austrian peasants and one whose ancestry could be traced back over a thousand years, but it worked because both parties wanted something from the other: Hitler desired that Britain should stay out of the affairs of Germany on the Continent and the Duke wanted his wife to be acknowledged and, if possible, his throne restored to him. As they left that October afternoon, Hitler remarked to his interpreter, Dr Paul Schmidt, 'That woman should have been queen.' It was exactly what both parties hoped to achieve.

Three months after the successful completion of the Venlo Operation the German Ambassador to the Netherlands wrote to von Ribbentrop saying that his letter was for the Führer's personal attention and 'Through personal relationships I might have the opportunity to establish certain lines to the Duke of Windsor'. He stated that the Duke was unhappy with his present position as a senior liaison officer with the French and, more importantly, 'There seems to be the beginning of a Fronde forming around W. When he was recently in London, I had explained to him through an intermediary why it is completely utopian for England to attempt a change of regime in Germany, and the statements of my intermediary are believed to have made a certain impression on him.'

From this letter it is clear (a) that the Germans felt they could still talk openly to a general in the British Army and a national of a country at war with Germany, and (b) that appeasement was not dead. The same people who had wanted to do a deal with the 'German resistance', if that was what it was, at Venlo, were still eager to continue those treacherous contacts with the enemy.

Over the next few months the Ambassador and others were able to report to von Ribbentrop, the German Foreign Minister, on other statements made by the Duke, which seemed to make it clear he was opposed to the continuation of the war with Germany and wouldn't be disinclined to make some deal with Hitler that would stop it before the fighting got out of hand.

But then events overtook the Windsors. On 10 May, 1940, Hitler marched westwards into the Low Countries and France. Panic followed. Sixteen days later the Foreign Secretary, Lord Halifax, suggested to the War Cabinet: 'The issue is not so much . . . a question of imposing a complete defeat on Germany but on safeguarding the Empire.'

Peace, it seemed, was in the air. But the appeasers hadn't reckoned with the new Prime Minister, Winston Churchill. Two days later he told his cabinet: 'The only way we can get back [into Europe] is by showing the world that Germany has not beaten us. . . . Let us therefore avoid being dragged down the slippery slope with France.'

It was not a sentiment that appealed to the Duke of Windsor. In that very week he deserted from the British Army! Without permission, he left his staff job and took Wallis to the South of France. They travelled south in a small fleet of heavily laden cars down roads jammed with French and Belgian refugees heading for the coast. They ended up at Biarritz, once famous for its casinos and high living, now the closest 'smart' town to the border with neutral Spain.

On 19 June the Duke's small entourage crossed into Spain. The Germans, who had excellent contacts in that country, especially Admiral Canaris of the *Abwehr*, who spent as much time as possible in Spain, were immediately aware of the Windsors' presence. Von Stohrer, the German Ambassador, at once cabled von Ribbentrop seeking advice as to how the

Windsors should be treated. He asked whether 'we might be interested in detaining the Duke here and eventually maintaining contact with him'. Von Ribbentrop replied the next day: 'Is it possible . . . to detain the Duke and Duchess of Windsor before they are granted an exit visa?' Ribbentrop always had an eye for the main chance. If he could use the Windsors to bring about peace between Germany and Britain it would be a tremendous coup for him.

But before the Germans in Spain could act the Windsors suddenly left for Portugal to take up residence at Estoril at the home of the banker Dr Ricardo Espiritu Santo e Silva, who, despite his name, was a Jew, a friend of the Rothschilds *and* a Nazi sympathizer. After all, he owned a private bank in a totalitarian state and he had to look after his family interests.

It was a foolish place to have taken up even temporary residence while Churchill decided what post the 'deserter' might take up next. The villa was isolated and easily accessible. But that didn't particularly worry the Duke, for as, David Eccles, who was then working for the Ministry of Economic Warfare in Lisbon, wrote to his wife, 'The Duke is pretty Fifth Column', and the fact that German, Italian, Portugese, Spanish and British agents were watching the place didn't present a problem for him. It was quite clear that the Windsors weren't sure whether they would leave Europe or not. That summer, in fact, the Duke was faced by the second most important decision of his life.

If he went along with Churchill, always one of his well-wishers, and let himself be moved out of supposed influence of the Nazis, where would he go? It certainly wouldn't be back to England. Queen Elizabeth, who blamed the Windsors for having forced her unwilling husband to ascend the throne after the Abdication, wouldn't tolerate that. Naturally the Army brass wouldn't now let him take up any military command. That left the relative obscurity of the Empire and there all the key posts were in the hands of capable, clever men.

The alternative was to remain behind and think the unthinkable, collaboration with Hitler and his return to the throne of Britain, with Wallis as Queen at his side.

That seems to have been von Ribbentrop's thinking too. For one morning in July, 1940, Ribbentrop's 'sonorous voice' came over the telephone at Schellenberg's Berlin office: 'Tell me, my dear fellow, could you come over to my office at once? You have time, haven't you?'

Schellenberg did have time.

4

Schellenberg, who by now knew his chief's strengths and weaknesses, decided to report the conversation immediately. For Heydrich was, as he wrote after the war, 'pathologically jealous'. Heydrich took the information fairly calmly. He contented himself with, 'I see; the old gentleman no longer wishes to consult me. Well, go over there and give him my best regards.' With that Schellenberg was dismissed.

Ribbentrop received Schellenberg standing behind his desk, as was normal. Pleasantries were exchanged and then Ribbentrop got down to business. 'The crux of the matter is that, since his abdication, the Duke has been under strict surveillance by the British Secret Service. It's almost as if he is a prisoner. And we know from our reports that he still entertains the same sympathetic feelings towards Germany and that, given the right circumstances, he wouldn't be averse to escaping from his present environment, and if he did go [to Spain] he'd be ready to be friends with Germany again. The Führer thinks this attitude is very important.'

Schellenberg must have realized that he was on to something very big and very dangerous. He listened as Ribbentrop went on to say that the Führer was prepared to pay the Duke 50 million Swiss francs, 'if he were ready to make some official gesture disassociating himself from the manoeuvres of the British Royal Family'.

In other words, Hitler was offering the former King a fortune not just for the sake of 'disassociating himself' from George VI, but, more importantly, for openly declaring himself for peace and a plea to be restored to the British throne. For nearly two centuries the Hanoverian rulers of Britain had been notorious for their greed and The Duke was no exception; he was an expert at letting other people pay his bills. But never once had a Hanoverian been prepared to betray his country for money.

Now the matter was in the open, Ribbentrop filled Schellenberg in (and Heydrich, for the conversation was immediately reported to the latter) on what he expected him to do. He was to establish contact with the Duke. The money was to be made ready and the Duke invited to cross the border to Spain where SD agents could keep a closer watch on him.

Schellenberg might have been something of a coward but he was nobody's fool. He wanted to know exactly where he stood in this matter. He asked, 'Do I understand that, if the Duke of Windsor should resist, I am to bring him in by force?'

Ribbentrop considered. He liked to be seen 'considering'. He felt that it gave him the kind of gravitas that went with his high office. 'Well,' the Foreign Minister said finally, 'the Führer feels that force should be used primarily against the British Secret Service.'

It was about then that their conversation was broken by a call from no less a person than the Führer himself. Schellenberg pretended not to hear, but naturally he strained his ears to catch every word. According to his later account, the Führer did not seem particularly happy with the Ribbentrop plan. But in the end he heard Ribbentrop say, 'Very well then, Schellenberg will fly by special plane to Madrid as soon as possible.' Faintly he heard Hitler reply, 'Tell him from me that I am relying on him.'

Ribbentrop rose, bowed to the telephone and intoned solemnly, 'Thank you, *mein Führer.*'

In other circumstances Schellenberg would have found the gesture funny, but not now, when his own life might be on the line. But Hitler was not quite finished. He added a codicil which showed that he had assessed the Windsors' marriage correctly: 'Schellenberg should particularly bear in mind the importance of the Duchess's attitude and try as hard as possible to gain her support. She has the greatest influence over the Duke.'

So it started. Naturally the whole truth of what went on in the Iberian peninsula that July will never be known. Schellenberg's account was dictated under duress. The SIS certainly have some of the relevant documents under lock and key, and naturally the British Royal Family, however much they hated Wallis, made sure that there was a thorough cleaning up after them in 1945. The arch-traitor Anthony Blunt, and many like him, though they weren't traitors, swarmed all over the Continent seizing papers, documents and the like recording high-level and treacherous contacts between Britain and Germany throughout the war via neutral countries such as Switzerland and Spain.

It seemed that a three-sided secret war took place between Heydrich's agents, the British SIS and Churchill, who wanted the Duke out of Europe before he could do any more damage to the British cause, and the Windsors who didn't want to go. What is not clear is whether the Duke, under the influence of Wallis, was really trying to cook up some deal with Hitler which would restore him to the throne before Churchill grabbed him by the neck and dragged him from the Continent.

While this strange game was going on in the south, Heydrich, nominally in charge of the operation, was making his own plans for the Duke's native country. Now that Operation Sealion, as the invasion of Britain was code-named, was in the final planning stage, Heydrich couldn't resist getting involved in it. As his wife complained, 'Reinhard was always looking for new tasks. Unfortunately when he found them, he couldn't bring himself to relinquish his old ones.'

As next in command to Himmler, he knew it would be his job to round up anyone regarded as dangerous to the Third Reich once Britain had been taken over. So his specialists, under the command of Dr Six, who would be the SD's representative in Britain, had a 'black list' drawn up. This would be used by the Gestapo as the basis for the immediate arrest of the persons mentioned. (Later Schellenberg claimed in his memoirs that he

90. **Cooper, Ivor,** Mitgl. d. brit. Rüstungsausschusses, London, The Old School House, Rudgewick (Sussex), RSHA III D 2.
91. **Copeland, Fred,** RSHA VI G 1.
92. **Coralfleet, Pierre,** richtig: Frank Davison, vermutl. England, RSHA IV E 4.
93. **Cormack, Georges,** Direktor, zuletzt Riga, vermutl. England, RSHA IV E 4.
94. **Coudenhove-Calerghi, Richard,** 17.11.94 Tokio, Schriftsteller, vermutl. England (Österr. Legitimist), RSHA IV A 6.
95. **Courboin,** brit. Agent, zuletzt Brüssel, vermutl. England, RSHA IV E 4.
96. **Coward, Noel,** vermutl. London, RSHA VI G 1.
97. **Mc. Cracken, C.,** 18.7.60 London, brit. Oberleutn., zuletzt Brüssel vermutl. England, RSHA IV E 4.
97ᵃ **Craig, Noel,** 11.11.86, zuletzt Kopenhagen, vermutl. England, RSHA IV E 4.
98. **Cranborne, R.,** Unterstaatssekretär, England, RSHA VI G 1.
99. **Crawford, Janet,** 14.4.77, zuletzt Bukarest, vermutl. England, RSHA IV E 4.
100. **Crawford,** Leiter d. brit. ND., zuletzt Athen, vermutl. England, RSHA IV E 4.
101. **Creighton, T. M.,** vermutl. England (Täterkreis: Algernon Slade) RSHA IV E 4.
102. **Crick, Siegfried,** 40 Jahre alt, England, Deckname: Krik, RSHA IV E. 4.
103. **Cripps, Sir Stafford,** Botschafter in Moskau, London E. C. 4, 8 Elm Court, Temple, RSHA II B 4, VI G 1.
104. **Cromwell, William,** England, RSHA IV E 4.
105. **Crook,** Angehöriger des brit. ND., England, RSHA IV E 4.
106. **Crossfield, B. P.,** 1882, Direktor der New Chronicle, RSHA VI G 1.
107. **Crossman, R. H. S.,** RSHA VI G 1.
108. **Crowther, Goffrey,** 1907, Direktor, England, RSHA VI G 1.
109. **Crozier, W. P.,** Hauptschriftleiter England, RSHA VI G 1.
110. **Cummings, A. J.,** Mitarb. d. News Chronicle, RSHA IV B 4, VI G 1
111. **Cunard, Nancy,** England, RSHA VI G 1.
112. **Curitz, David Nathaniel,** Wohnung: Cardiff, Four Winds Pensisely Rd. RSHA II B 2.
113. **Curnbull, John,** England (Täterkreis: Stevens/Best), RSHA IV E 4.
114. **Curtis, Frederick P. C., Dr.,** Privatdozent, vermutl. England, RSHA III A 1.
115. **Czogalla, Stanislaus, Dr.,** 28.4.98 Zawade b. Ratibor, Vertreter, vermutl. England, RSHA IV E 5, Stapo Oppeln.
116. **Czoska, August,** 1.4.85 Soppischin, poln. Zollinspektor, vermutl. England, RSHA IV E 5, Stapo Graudenz.

When this list was published in 1945, Rebecca West, who was on it, wired Noel Coward 'My dear, the people we would have been seen dead with!'

had produced the list, but this seems hardly likely as he was in Spain for most of that period.) The list included people long dead, others who had hurriedly departed to the Dominions at the outbreak of the war and such convinced anti-Nazis as Noel Coward and the social luminary, Nancy Cunard.

Heydrich's office also produced another interesting guide *Informationsheft GB* – Information Booklet GB. It was intended to help the leather-coated 'heavies' of the German Secret Police in their search for loot and traditional sources of anti-German feeling in Britain. High among the latter was, of course, Eton and the other great public schools. They 'deserve special attention,' as the Guide noted. 'Vital anti-German propaganda is to be found there.' After remarking that 'Eton is booked up to the year 1949'* and commenting on the strange increase of ex-public schoolboys in Major Attlee's Labour Party, the unknown compiler of the *Informationsheft* concluded, 'The whole system is calculated to rear men of inflexible will and ruthless energy who regard intellectual problems as a waste of time, but know human nature and how to dominate other men in the most unscrupulous fashion.'

Similar surveys were produced on the Roman Catholic church, the Buchmanite Oxford Movement, even the Boy Scout Movement. Naturally Jews and communists came in for special treatment; Heydrich, with his usual thoroughness, had had the number of British Jews calculated down to the nearest hundred. In the guide's estimation there were over 300,000. Naturally, due to the Führer's own obsession with the machinations of the Freemasons, there was a long account of the British lodges, plus a detailed, if rubbishy, study of the British Intelligence Service. This was another obsession of Hitler's, who always maintained that 'What we need is something like the British Secret Service – an order doing its work with passion'.

---

* One wonders if the compiler of the guide received this information from von Ribbentrop. For when the latter was German Ambassador to the Court of St James before the war, he tried to get his son, Rudolf, into Eton, but was told it was 'full'. Instead he sent him to Westminster. Thus that London public school has the doubtful honour of having an old boy who served in the elite 1st SS.

Today it is easy to smile at the mistakes, the naivety and real lack of understanding of the British mentality in these 'guides'. But they did represent something of an achievement. They had been conceived and printed in a matter of weeks (this is evidenced by the use of statements made in German captivity by Best and Stevens, kidnapped the previous November). With all their faults and misinterpretations, they were well prepared under great pressure and would be in the hands of German staff officers by August, 1940. (Five months earlier, when the Germans had prepared to invade Norway, the German ground commander had been forced to go out and buy a Baedeker guide with his own money because of the lack of information about that country!)

Again Heydrich, with typical energy, which would soon be used for a project of much greater magnitude and one which would blacken Germany's name for the rest of the 20th Century, had fought time and the normal slowness of office-bound bureaucrats to produce what Peter Fleming has described as 'A complete set of documents – the maps, photographs, street-plans, topographical date, tables translating yards into metres and shillings into marks, summaries of British constitutional history and all the rest of it – large enough to fill a small haversack.' He concluded that, 'Those who ordered this work to be done and those, who in a very short time, did, can hardly be dismissed as dilettantes.'* Fleming was right. *Obergruppenführer* Reinhard Heydrich could hardly have been called a dilettante.

* Peter Fleming, *Invasion 1940*, (Rupert Hart-Davis, 1957).

5

While Heydrich ran Germany's police forces and prepared, on the side, for his role in Operation Sealion, he tried to keep control of the confused situation in the Iberian Peninsula. *'Unternehmen Willi'*, as the Schellenberg operation was called, with 'Willi' standing for 'Windsor', was facing problems caused not only by the SIS, attached to the British Embassy in Madrid, by Churchill in London and by the local authorities, who were, on the whole, trying to keep both sides happy, but also by the Duke himself. Suddenly he seemed to be playing a double game. While trying to keep an increasingly angry Churchill at bay by promising to leave Europe as soon as transport was available, he was also still in contact with the Germans.

Through von Stohrer, he thanked Ribbentrop for securing his Paris house in the occupied French capital (and also his bank account, though he didn't mention that). He also informed the German Foreign Minister that Churchill was threatening to have him court-martialled if he didn't take up the post the Prime Minister had offered him as Governor of the Bahamas. At the same time he was infuriating the hard-pressed Churchill with such trivia as whether he could have a Scots Guardsman as his batman if he left for Nassau and requesting that his favourite cigarettes and tobacco should be dispatched from London to Lisbon *by the next flying boat*!

Meanwhile Schellenberg was going ahead with his own plans to suborn the Duke or, if necessary, kidnap him. Through a Japanese agent (yet another complication in this complicated

51

story) he obtained the plans and other details of the Duke's home in Estoril borrowed by the undecided couple from the Nazis' Jewish agent. All the servants were bribed and from now on not a single word uttered by the Duke went unreported. Schellenberg even managed to replace the Portugese guards with his own people. His unlimited financial resources opened all doors. But would they seduce the Duke into coming over into the German camp before it was too late and Churchill had him shipped off to the other side of the world?

Schellenberg decided to force the Duke's hand. Together, he and the Jap agent sneaked into the grounds of the Duke's home (again, the guards had been bribed) and started throwing stones at the windows. Their intention was make the Windsors nervous. Immediately the guards turned out and began an intensive search of the grounds for the 'assailants'. Next morning the bribed servants told their master and mistress that the mysterious stone throwing had been the work of the perfidious 'English Secret Service'. The Duke's comments are not recorded, but a few days later Schellenberg stepped up the pressure by having a bouquet of flowers delivered at the house with a note saying: 'Beware of the machinations of the British Secret Service – a Portugese friend who has your best interests at heart'.

Now, however, it was Schellenberg's turn to begin to feel vulnerable in Portugal. His Japanese agent told him that he, was being shadowed by men of the SIS. He wasn't, but from now on Schellenberg played the role of a fictional spy to the hilt, 'altering my route, changing from bus to taxi,' and the like. But he simply couldn't shake off his shadows – or so he thought. After the war he learned from his Secret Service interrogators that they 'did not even know that I was in Portugal'. That must have been a great let down for Schellenberg with his vivid imagination and sense of his own importance.

Meanwhile his reports to Berlin were not receiving the attention he felt they deserved. For the time being Heydrich was too busy with the plans for the invasion of Britain to be all that concerned with *Operation Willi*. It seemed that Ribbentrop was running the operation and his replies to Schellenberg's communications had 'grown cooler and cooler'. Then, out of

1. "Arrogant, haughty and cold-eyed, Heydrich seemed to put the fear of death into all with whom he had dealings" (p.viii).

2. Alfred Naujocks, "the man who was to start the Second World War" (p.1). This photograph was taken afer the war when he was a bouncer in a brothel in Hamburg.

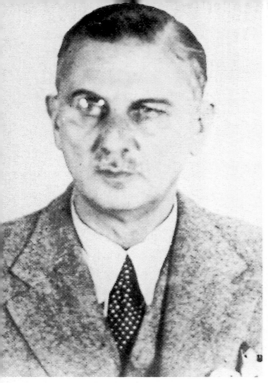 

3 & 4. "Two military men of the old school, Captain Payne Best and Major Stevens" (p.27).

5. "Walter Schellenberg was another of Heydrich's 'intellectual gangsters' " (p.28).

6. Klop's "knees began to buckle beneath him. Slowly he fell to the ground in a pool of his own blood" (p. 34).

7. The conference room at the Berghof, where Hitler hoodwinked Neville Chamberlain over the fate of Czechoslovakia.

8. "She was neither pretty, intelligent nor British" (p.41). The Prince of Wales, as he then was, with Mrs Simpson at Fort Belvedere in 1935.

9. "Himmler was very much concerned with the racial purity question" (p.69).

10. "Eichmann... came up with a ready answer. It was to make certain Jews honorary members of the SS!" (p. 87).

the blue, he got a telegram from the Foreign Minister which read: 'The Führer orders that an abduction [of the Windsors] be organized at once.' That must have been a shock for Schellenberg, but he knew he had to obey, whatever the risk.

In the end he turned to his Japanese 'friend', who has always remained nameless. He listened to what Schellenberg had to say, remarked that the Führer must know what he was about and then added slyly, 'But what do you really want to discuss with me? How to carry out this order, or how to evade it?' Schellenberg had been rumbled. Naturally he didn't want to risk his own skin. He blustered a little but the Jap brushed his words to one side and said, 'How you will justify yourself to the Führer is not my affair. Let us not lose any more time, but discuss how you can circumvent the order.' It was a sentiment with which Schellenberg agreed wholeheartedly. He shut up and listened.

The Jap's solution was simple: warn the British, *indirectly*, about what was afoot. He would bribe his 'friend' at Portugese police headquarters to increase the number of policemen guarding the Duke. The reason given to the Duke would be that the locals suspected that he might be kidnapped by the British Secret Service. At the same time this greatly increased number of police guards, thirty in all, would make it clear to Ribbentrop that Schellenberg had little chance of getting through them to the Duke.

The plan started working almost as soon as it was put into force. Ambassador Stohrer reported to the German Foreign Minister that 'In Portugal [the Duke] feels almost like a prisoner. He is surrounded by agents. . . .' He went on to tell Ribbentrop that the Duke felt ever more distant from the King and from Churchill's government, but that the Windsors had less to fear from the King, who 'is quite foolish'. But the 'shrewd Queen' was quite a different kettle of fish. 'She was intriguing skilfully against the Duke and in particular against the Duchess.'

Meanwhile Schellenberg's machinations behind the scenes were worrying not only Churchill but also President Roosevelt. His representatives in Portugal felt certain that an attempt was to be made by the Germans to capture the Duke, and Roosevelt knew that if the Duke of Windsor declared for the Nazis that would dash his hopes of ever bringing America into the war on Britain's side.

Thus it was that in the last week of July, 1940, the activities of these two pleasure-loving exiles affected the destinies of nations. Now both Roosevelt and Churchill started to put the pressure on the Duke of Windsor. Hitler countered by informing the Windsors' host – indirectly of course – that he was willing to co-operate with the Duke in any future alliance between Germany and Britain. At the same time he warned the Duke that, once he left Portugal for the Bahamas, if he did, Churchill would keep the couple there permanently in order to have complete control over them.

But the Duke was not ready openly to declare his support for Hitler at a time when the latter was actively preparing to invade Britain; that would make him out all too plainly to be the opportunist traitor which indeed he was. He informed Churchill that he was prepared to go to the Bahamas as 'a temporary solution', since it appeared that his brother and sister-in-law were not prepared to bring the family feud to an end. In the middle of a world war the Duke was mostly preoccupied with family feuding! It was typical of the man.

Schellenberg was beginning to relax. The Japanese plan was working. He reported that little could be done with the Duke, who, although he wished fervently to remain in Europe, was being threatened with assassination by the British Secret Service if he did so. A bomb had been reported, for instance, in the hold of the ship scheduled to take him to the Bahamas. Whether true or false, the bomb scare caused great alarm. The Portugese authorities searched the ship from stem to stern. Schellenberg was delighted when the police, apparently not satisfied with the results of the first search, repeated the exercise. As he wrote in his memoirs, 'Security measures were doubled, then redoubled; everything helped to confirm my reports to Berlin on the impossibility of carrying out the abduction.'

By now it was clear that the Windsors would have to go and Hitler and Ribbentrop stopped putting on pressure at the diplomatic level. Schellenberg's plans to kidnap the Duke were dropped. The British Secret Service rapidly gained control over the situation and censored the Duke's every movement, though a score or so of people in Lisbon knew when he would sail in the *SS Excalibur*. It was not surprising. Other rats from Anglo-American high society, who had wasted their lives – and fortunes – for years in the South of France and other European waterholes were getting out while the going was good.

The Duke kept on procrastinating, however. He tried to stay the *Excalibur*'s departure for a further week but the move failed. On 1 August, 1940, he went on board. The next day the ship sailed. A plane, in which was Baron Eugene de Rothschild, swooped in low to see them off. It was ironic. One wonders how long the Baron would have lasted if the Hitler-Windsor deal had come off. That night the Windsors, after an afternoon of sunbathing on the First Class deck, were entertained by the Biddles, he until recently US ambassador to Poland. It was all very jolly and relaxed. The Windsors might well have been on a peacetime holiday cruise. In fact they were going into exile for good.

Schellenberg watched them go through his field glasses. The ship was so close, he recorded, that 'I seemed almost able to touch it. . . . Slowly I returned to my house. The chapter was closed.'

It was and he had survived. Back in Berlin he reported to Ribbentrop, who excused himself early, as if he were sick of the whole business. That afternoon he drove over to the Prinz Albrechtstrasse to report to Heydrich, who took everything very calmly. He listened quietly, nodded several times and finally said, 'A rather disjointed affair. Please don't get yourself involved too closely with Ribbentrop. I feel that you should not have accepted this assignment from the beginning. Obviously you must have realized from the start how it would probably end. I must say that you carried it off rather shrewdly.'

Thus ended the aptly named Operation Willi. After he had dismissed Schellenberg that afternoon Heydrich must have thought that the *Englandspiel* was over for good. The British had retreated back to their foggy little island. He guessed he had seen the end of them. Now he could concentrate on the two vital operations that had begun to emerge, the Führer having gone cold on Operation Sealion.

But Heydrich was wrong. In the end the British were to be his nemesis. For in that same first week of August several hundred soldiers, dressed in shabby bits and pieces of British and French uniforms, and wearing forage caps that belonged to neither army, straggled from York station out of the town to the racecourse on the Knavesmire. They were obviously not British troops, for they were unarmed and their bearing was very sloppy. Neither were they Italian POWs, a few of whom had begun to be brought to the Knavesmire enclosure for 'enemy aliens'. These men were short and stocky and looked decidedly foreign.

They were the dissidents from a newly arrived foreign brigade just off boats from the South of France. Most of them had been in action before they had been evacuated, but they had mutinied when they landed. They complained that their officers were fascist and anti-semitic and they no longer wanted to fight with what was left of the Czech Division, set up by the French. Under the command of a former communist MP, Vladimir Clementis, one day to be post-war Czechoslovakia's Foreign Minister and hanged in 1952 after confessing to being a 'Western Imperialist', they had refused to bear arms.

The British authorities had acted quickly. The previous July Anthony Eden, the new Foreign Minister, had heard from senior British generals at a secret meeting in York's Station Hotel, outside the very station where the Czech dissidents had just arrived, that the average British conscript wouldn't fight if the Germans invaded; he would simply drift back home. The rot had to be stopped swiftly. So these 150 Czechs were discharged from the Czech Army and removed from their comrades by British redcaps armed with revolvers.

All in all not a very significant event, of interest only because among the mutineers who marched through York that day was a certain 17-year-old private who had adopted the name 'Jan Hoch'. In due course, when he was enrolled into the British Pioneer Corps, he took on yet another name, this time adopted from a popular cigarette of the time, 'du Maurier', before finally emerging into the world of big-time publishing as Robert Maxwell.

Heydrich would never learn of the existence of Maxwell, for by the time he began his rise to fame he would be long dead. But Heydrich would definitely hear of those loyal Czechs whom Maxwell had left behind at the Czech Brigade's new camp in the grounds of the castle at Cholmondeley just outside Whitchurch. For there two young Czechoslovak patriots, both sergeants, one a farmer from Moravia, the other a locksmith from Slovakia, were preparing to take their revenge on the Germans.

They had come a long way to this rural backwater, seemingly so far away from the war in Europe. It must have seemed like years to them since they had first gone on the run, with Heydrich's Gestapo on their heels. They had crossed the border of their own country as virtual outlaws, with every man's hand against them. Near Warsaw they had found a temporary refuge, but not for long. The two fugitives had been easy targets for the eager recruiters of the French Foreign Legion. Another lap in their long adventure had begun. They had been enrolled into that élite formation, made up of men without a country *and* without hope.

During the fighting in France, before the French authorities had disbanded their Czech Division after their defeat by the Germans, both men had won bravery awards. Now these two obscure Czech sergeants, Josef Gabcik and Jan Kubis, were going to take their revenge. They would kill the tyrant and enjoy their brief moment of fame.

III

INTERNATIONAL AFFAIRS

'Ye have scarce the soul of a louse,' he
said, 'but the roots of sin are there.'

Rudyard Kipling

1

Reichsmarshal Goering once exploded when questioned on the fact that one of his people was Jewish, *'I* shall decide who's Jewish or not here.' His outburst reflected a popular tendency in Hitler's Germany, even among high-ranking Party members. They all seemed, despite the Nuremberg Racial Laws, to have some sort of Jewish coterie around them. In Goering's case, for example, not only was his youthful protector a Jew and probably the lover of his neglected mother; the doctor who hid and attended him after he had been wounded in the 1923 Munich Putsch and his most senior air marshal, Field Marshal Milch, who was responsible for the four-month blitz on London in 1940/41 were also Jews.

As we know, there is no doubt that the Nazi Party and probably a large minority of the German people were anti-semitic. All the same, these very people went to Jewish doctors and dentists, did business with Jewish bankers, admired Jewish stars of stage and screen and had Jewish mistresses, even wives.

More than any other Western European country, Jews had been inextricably mixed in the life of Germany ever since they had emerged from the ghettoes at the end of the eighteenth century. Even such racial fanatics as Himmler seemed at ease with Jews and was not averse to dealing with the 'Hebrew spawn' as late as 1944. Even then, two years after he had reported proudly to his Führer that Germany was *judenrein* (pure of Jews), there were thousands of Jews still at large in the country. There were Jews passing as Aryans still working in German war industries, even Jews who won the Nazi *Kriegsverdienstkreuz* (the War Service Cross) for their efforts. Virtually everyone in Germany had Jewish associates and friends, even the country peasants who dealt with the *Pluenjuden*, the Jewish pedlars who sold their wares from great wickerwork baskets on their backs. But when these Jews started to disappear people of all classes, who might well have known nothing about the concentration camps, must have realized that something dreadful must have happened. *

But apart from perverted racist fanatics in the Nazi Party such as Julius Streicher, the publisher of the pornographic *Der Sturmer*, the Nazi *Prominenz* rarely seemed to make a personal issue of anti-semitism or the persecution of Jewish citizens. There was one major exception and that was the 'blond Jew', as he was known behind his back, Reinhard Heydrich.

The Jews for Heydrich were 'anti-social elements' (*Asozialen*), representatives of an international conspiracy, destined to destroy the 'Aryan' race, who had to be wiped out. Unlike Himmler, with his strange Aryan cults, based on German myths, perverted anthropology and secret Teutonic orders, Heydrich took a wholly pragmatic attitude to the Jews. If they couldn't be resettled elsewhere, they had to be exterminated.

At the beginning of the 'Thousand Year Reich', he had been instrumental in having long lists of Jews compiled, ready for the day when the Party ordered action to be taken against these 'anti-social elements'. In this manner his SS-SD *apparat* assumed a leading role in the *Judenfrage* (the Jewish question). But, following a few bad years for Germany's Jews after

---

* In the small town in S.W. Germany in which the author lived for several years they still tell the story of the funeral of the town's most prominent Jew in 1938 when virtually everyone turned out to accompany the coffin to the cemetery. The mourners *included all the local SS men*. To me this has always seemed indicative of just how German Jews were integrated into their society even during the savage excesses of the Nazi period.

1933, the 1936 Olympic Games, held in Germany, forced the Führer to relax the Party's persecution.

But that didn't stop Heydrich's constant monitoring of Jewish organizations. If the Jews could not be dealt with inside Germany, then they had to be got rid of by a combination of financial blackmail, expropriation and deportation. Here an obscure young Austrian, who spoke Yiddish and some Hebrew and had actually been to British-mandated Palestine, a new recruit to the SD, led the way. He was to be the first of the many of Heydrich's feared 'Jewish experts'.

Using the same kind of measures that the young Adolf Eichmann was beginning to apply in newly annexed Austria, Heydrich tried not only to force German Jews to leave their native land through threats, forced purchases of their homes and expropriation of their funds, but actually actively *helped* them to emigrate to the 'promised land'. Once he quipped that, 'One day the Chief Rabbi will have a statue of me erected in Jerusalem for what I've done for the Yids.'

At that time the British Mandate authorities, in a vain attempt to keep the peace and prevent the armed feuding between Palestine's Arabs and the new Jewish settlers from breaking into a full-scale war, had imposed a strict embargo on Jewish immigrants.* British agents were active everywhere in ports through which battered old charter ships might try to smuggle Jews illegally into Palestine; when such ships did try to land their pathetic human freight the Royal Navy stepped in and stopped them.

Pitted against the British in this undeclared war was the Jewish settlers' Haganah defence organization, which was also fighting to defend Jewish settlements against Arab attacks. In 1937 this organization had actually made contact with Heydrich's SD through an intermediary named Feifel Polkes. A year later two members of the same organization *apparently* (though in fact they were from the newly formed Jewish

* These kinds of bans on Jewish immigrants were applied virtually every-where in a Western World, just emerging from the Depression. Even America refused to take more than a nominal number of Jewish refugees from German persecution.

63

Intelligence outfit, Mossad) entered the lion's den, coming to Berlin to discuss with the SD ways of smuggling German Jews into Palestine *with* Heydrich's help! The mind boggles at the vision of the creator of the 'Final Solution' negotiating with the two agents, Pino Ginzburg and Moshe Auerbach!

At the same time that Jews were being shamefully abused, even beaten up publicly on the streets of Berlin, Ginzburg took up residence in the city to oversee the illegal transports to Palestine. Weekly, using Müller's men to do the rounding up when necessary, Heydrich supplied Ginzburg with 400 Berlin Jews for shipment to the Holy Land.

By October, 1939, Heydrich planned to allow the Mossad, which was paying for the operation, to send 'emigrants' directly from Hamburg and Emden, using the facilities of Canaris's *Abwehr* and the German Navy to ensure that the ships were not intercepted en route.

The attack on Poland and the British declaration of war on Germany on 3 September, 1939, brought an abrupt end to this bizarre co-operation between the would-be murderer and his victims. Suddenly Heydrich and his 'extermination groups' were fully occupied in Poland wiping out the Polish intelligentsia and the country's nearly one million Jews.

But by this time two-thirds of all Jews in Germany, Austria and Czechoslovakia had emigrated safely, with 70,000 alone reaching Palestine. Still, Heydrich had calculated that there were still eleven million Jews in Europe (including 300,000 in Britain) to be dealt with before the continent was free of the 'Hebrew bacillus'. How was he going to do it? Genocide, as far as we know, had not been considered by mid-1940. The Jews had to be cleared out of Europe by other means. But if Palestine under the British didn't want them and Germany certainly didn't, where should they go?

Now, after the fall of France, Heydrich resurrected an old idea for dealing with the problem. It had first been mooted back in 1927 by a Dutchman, Egon van Winghenes, in Rotterdam, who had suggested that an island such as the French colony of Madagascar would be an ideal 'home' into which 'world Jewry' could be resettled. Naturally, he didn't ask whether they wanted to be taken from New York, London or Berlin and dumped in the middle of the Indian Ocean. Such 'visionaries' never have much sense of humour. Here, according to Van Winghenes, it would be 'easy to control them' and 'reduce the danger of infection from the Jewish bacillus' to a minimum.

Winghenes put forward his theory under the guise of being a convinced Zionist – perhaps he had never heard of the old Jewish saying that 'a Zionist is a Jew who pays a second Jew to send a third Jew to Palestine' – and maintained that the Jewish race deserved a land sufficiently large in which to 'develop itself'.

Naturally Heydrich had read of Winghenes' idea. Now, with France defeated and with a French government prepared to accommodate the German victors in any way they could, he revived the Dutchman's suggestion. This time, however, the Jews wouldn't be *asked* to go; they would be shipped to Madagascar by force if necessary. There they would be 'given a sufficiently large area to form a Jewish state', naturally under Aryan (read 'German') control.

As always when Heydrich decided upon something, action started immediately. Eichmann was sent to Hamburg's Tropical Institute to learn about climatic conditions. Ribbentrop was contacted about the diplomatic steps involved and informed that some four million Jews would probably be resettled there after the war, which most German leaders thought, with only Britain left in the conflict, would be soon, perhaps a matter of months. Some one or two thousand Jews were shoved over the Reich's borders into France, presumably as forerunners of these 'Zionist settlers', though naturally they had no idea they had been selected for this happy fate.

Later students of the 'Final Solution' would maintain that the 'Madagascar Proposal' was, in reality, only a cover for the mass extermination of the Jews soon to come. But, as cynical and cruel as Heydrich was, in 1940 he had not the means of mass extermination needed to liquidate an estimated eleven million European Jews. He really intended to force through a mass exodus, cleansing the continent of their presence for good.

But that wasn't to be. Another and greater problem now started to loom on the horizon which overshadowed the *Judenfrage*. With France knocked out of the war and Britain likely to surrender at any moment, Hitler now turned his attention to that country which he had always regarded as Germany's and Europe's, real and most dangerous enemy – Soviet Russia.

2

Thus, for a while, the Jewish Question was shelved and the Madagascar Solution vanished, to become a mere footnote to the history of the Second World War. Heydrich limited himself to the extermination of Polish intellectuals, officers and Jews of importance. At the same time, however, Jews were being collected throughout Germany and Occupied Europe to be sent to the new ghettoes being created in Poland, and afterwards in the newly conquered Eastern territories.

Later it was suggested that this assembling of Jews in areas where they could be readily controlled was a necessary prelude to their extermination. But such contemporary German records as are still available for the period of 1940/41 seem to indicate that Heydrich and his henchmen who were responsible for the Jews didn't really know what to do with them. Did you shoot them or imprison them? But where was the German manpower to come from to carry out either course? Already SS concentration camp guards in the Reich were being called up or conscripted into *Waffen SS* fighting units being readied for the attack on Russia. There was a financial problem too. Naturally confiscated Jewish property in the West had proved useful in filling the coffers of Himmler's *Allgemeine SS*. But that money was running out rapidly and the SS, unlike the military, had to pay for the services it required to maintain these hundreds of thousands of unproductive Jews now being established in the Eastern ghettoes and camps.

Great German firms, many of which exist to this day, were not prepared to give their assistance and advice simply for the glory of serving the holy cause of National Socialism. Himmler may well have made three directors of Germany's second leading bank, the Dresdner Bank, honorary colonels in the SS; the bank, which was already making enormous profits out of the war, wanted its pound of flesh too. It had advanced money to buy the land for the concentration camps and wanted interest on that money. *Die Allianzversicherung*, even today one of Europe's greatest insurance companies, had insured the camps. Now they, too, wanted their premiums paid. In time these premiums would amount to millions of reichsmarks yearly. And it was the same with dozens of other German firms, large and small, from local bakeries to massive building companies, which serviced the Jewish camps. Even the land-fill companies in whose sites Jews and other prisoners were given mass burials wanted to be paid. Dead or alive, the Jews were costing money, and money was running out.

The time had come, Heydrich realized, for a change of attitude. The problem couldn't be exported, not for the moment at least. They couldn't be liquidated; the SS didn't have the resources, the men, even the space, to get rid of the corpses. Somehow or other, with SS debts mounting rapidly due to the ever-increasing numbers of Jews being arrested and imprisoned, a way had to be found to make the Jews pay for their own incarceration. Heydrich himself had no answer to the problem, but there were others in the SD waiting in the wings to be summoned and prepared to put their cynical theories into practice when the time came, totally unconcerned by the fact that, in so doing, they would ruin Germany's moral reputation for generations to come. It would be these young men, the technocrats of death, the economists of genocide, who would transform Germany from the nineteenth century concept of being the home of *Dichter und Denker* (Poets and Thinkers) into the twentieth century's *Richter und Henker* (Judges and Hangmen).

While Heydrich and his associates pondered over the problem, and the war with Russia started with tremendous victories on the part of the *Wehrmacht*, victories which seemed to overshadow all the other problems facing the new masters of Europe, Schellenberg kept up his relationship with Canaris, the head of the rival secret service, *the Abwehr*.

One morning, upset after an RAF bombing raid on Berlin which had slightly damaged his flat, Schellenberg was not in a particularly receptive mood when, over their weekly breakfast, Canaris asked, 'Has *Obergruppenführer* Heydrich submitted any material on the Japanese to the Führer?'

Schellenberg was surprised at the depth of Canaris' knowledge of Heydrich's affairs and suspected Canaris might well have a mole in the Prinz Albrechtstrasse*. He replied, 'No, not as far as I know. But I do know that Himmler is very interested in Japan. In fact, before the Russian campaign he ordered that certain SS cadets were to learn Japanese. His idea was to send forty of them to serve in the Japanese Army and we were to have forty Japanese cadets serving with us.'

All the same, Schellenberg went on, Himmler was still very much concerned with the racial purity question. Even though the Japanese were 'honorary Aryans' the *Reichsführer SS* had strongly objected when one of the Japanese Embassy staff in Berlin had wanted to marry a German girl.

Still, as Japan and America slid ever closer to outright war, Himmler and Hitler started to relax their racially prejudiced attitude somewhat and it was now that an emissary from the East turned up in Berlin who wanted both Japanese *and* German help in freeing his 'occupied' country, and by no stretch of the imagination could this man be turned into an 'honorary Aryan'.

He was a high-caste Hindu who had been educated in England and, after a brief flirtation with communism, had become a diehard Indian nationalist. He was a fat bespectacled ex-member of the Congress Party in his late thirties. His name was Subhas Chandra Bose, known throughout his short life

---

* All the Party bigshots, spied on each other. Most of them realized that Hitler played them off against one another and it was wise to know one's rival's plans.

in the enemy public eye as 'the Tiger of India'.

In return for Hitler's help, Bose proposed that he should raise an 'Indian Legion' of some 3,000 men, to be recruited from Indians captured in North Africa and now imprisoned in German POW camps in the Reich. These men could be used as a regular fighting force once they had been trained by German officers and NCOs. Hitler disliked the idea: 'How can you make a man kill,' he snorted, 'who will remove even a beetle from his path rather than step on it?' So Bose suggested that it would be better if his 'Indian Legion' was employed in clandestine operations. They would feel they were doing something for their country if they were to fight as reconnaissance-and-sabotage units on India's North-West Frontier. A realist might have said, 'Yes, and from there they would have a better chance of desertion back to their native villages.' But Hitler sanctioned the move and so it was that, in an extremely racially prejudiced Germany, the first volunteers were moved to a training camp at Koenigsbruck just outside Dresden. The 'Indian Legion' had been born. It was going to be the first of many such 'non-Aryan' formations, including Bosnian Moslems, slant-eyed Tartars, even shaman-dominated Siberians, who sought admittance to the German Armed Forces, primarily those of the *Waffen SS* under the control of that Aryan fanatic Heinrich Himmler!

In the end Bose became dissatisfied with the Germans' reluctant efforts to help him free India. In 1942 he left Germany by U-boat, was picked up in mid-ocean by a Japanese submarine and transferred his support to the Japanese. But unfortunately they were as racially prejudiced as the Germans and had little time for the 'black coolies'. But they concealed their prejudices better. A 'Free Indian Army' was formed under the aegis of the Japanese-created Oriental 'Co-Prosperity Sphere' to fight in Burma. The several Indian divisions formed didn't do so well there and it was said that British officers had to forcibly restrain their men, especially the Gurkhas from executing the 'renegades' on the spot when they were captured.

The 3,000-man-strong Division *Freies Indien* trained by the Germans didn't do too well either when it finally went into action against regular troops in Normandy. Most of them surrendered, after a brief fight, to the Americans. As for Bose, his plane crashed at the end of the war in the Far East and his body was never recovered. Some said that he was trying to fly to Russia to re-start his campaign with yet another dictator as a new ally, namely Josef Stalin. But that might well be just a rumour.

Today, S.C.Bose is practically a forgotten man outside India. There, thirty years ago an equestrian statue was erected to the founder of the *Jai Hind* movement. It shows him mounted on a horse with an enormous tail, dressed in a very British-looking forage cap and wartime battledress, wearing, rather strangely for such an heroic pose, horn-rimmed glasses!

But the Indians and their problems were not one of Heydrich's priorities that autumn of 1941. Despite all the burdens of his office, he was determined to promote his own career and at the same time enjoy himself. Although he had been grounded after crashing the Me.109 fighter the year before, he still continued to fly his own antiquated 'double-decker' and, whenever he could, sneak off and fly the newer planes of the *Luftwaffe*.

In the confusion of the Eastern Front, where huge battles were being fought over vast areas, it was not so difficult for the 37-year-old SS Police General and Luftwaffe *Major der Reserve* to convince local Air Force authorities that he should play a small part in the new campaign. The mind boggles at the thought, but here was Himmler's second-in-command, who knew most of the Reich's greatest secrets, being allowed to fly missions behind the Russian front. But it was typical of Heydrich. The consequences of his actions didn't particularly worry him, as long as the action itself furthered his career. Indeed Heydrich was motivated solely by expediency and his own burning ambition, which one day, he thought, might well take him to the top. As he once told two cronies when drunk, he would not hesitate to get rid of Hitler himself if 'the old man makes a mess of things.'

But before he set out on the final and fatal stage of his meteoric career, Heydrich indulged himself one last time. Without informing Himmler, he persuaded the *Luftwaffe* authorities in the east to let him fly a reconnaissance-bombing mission behind the retreating Russians. Now, sixty years later, the details are vague. But what is known is that the second most feared man in Europe – after Himmler – was forced down and posted as missing.

Now the balloon went up. One can imagine the accusations and counter-accusations flying back and forth at the Eastern HQ of the *Luftwaffe*. Heads rolled. Staff officers were suddenly posted to front-line outfits. Infantry and reconnaissance units were despatched hastily to the general area where Heydrich's plane had been last reported. But they found nothing.

Then, suddenly, an unshaven, exhausted, but triumphant Heydrich turned up. For forty-eight hours he had wandered behind the enemy's line, dodging Russian patrols and skirting villages, stealing drinks out of wells and fruit off trees, until he finally reached the safety of his own lines.

One can imagine the collective sigh of relief that went up. One can imagine, too, Himmler's surprise when he spotted yet another medal on Heydrich's chest. Where had his subordinate won the Iron Cross, the Pilot's Combat Metal and the Wound Medal in Black when all he could bear on his skinny breast were the Sports Medal in bronze and the War Service Cross, Third Class?

But there was no time to answer the questions which might have satisfied his curiosity. For Heydrich had been given yet another task, in addition to all the other jobs he had, and he had accepted it with alacrity. It would mean that he would have to leave Berlin for weeks, perhaps months. But that didn't worry him, and the move certainly brought a sense of relief to many of his subordinates. At last, he told his wife, 'I'm no longer going to be the nation's damned bloodhound. It will change my life.'

It certainly would. In nine months' time he would be dead.

IV

FOUNDING AN ECONOMIC EMPIRE

*Am deutschen wesen soll die welt genesen**

*The world will thrive on Germany's nature.

Kaiser Wilhelm II

1

Drehscheiben German geo-politicians and military strategists call such places. It is a much more plastic and descriptive phrase than the somewhat prosaic English translation – 'turntables'.* It tends to cover the whole range of possibilities of the area – military, political and economic – in a way the English word doesn't.

In Central Europe, after the German invasion of Russia on 22 June, 1941, perhaps the most important of all those European *Drehscheiben* was that of Bohemia, formerly part of the Czechoslovakia Republic, but German since March, 1939. Anyone who possessed it could control the Baltic, the Danube, South-East Europe and the Central European waterways, plus the great weapon-producing Skoda Works at Pilsen and the Brünn Small Arms factory (where, incidentally, the British Army's standard light machine gun, the Bren, had been designed). In other words Bohemia was vitally important to the German war machine, more than ever so now, due to the war with Russia.

For just as the German victors had done in the occupied countries in the West, where the local bosses co-operated whole-heartedly with them, producing Renault tanks, French cannon, Belgian small arms, Dutch uniforms and so on, they

* The German verb *drehen* admittedly means 'to turn', but it also has the connotation of 'twisting' and 'fixing'.

now incorporated Czechoslovakian industry into their own war production. By September, 1941, the area, free from the danger of RAF bombing, was producing a third of the *Wehrmacht's* tanks, a quarter of all its trucks and forty per cent of its light machine guns; and ever more German war factories were moving into this bomb-free zone. Prague alone attracted 3000 German civil servants and office workers, plus their families, in two months between August and September that year.

But there was one fly in the ointment – the Czech government in exile in London under President Benes and its equivalent in Moscow led by Klement Gottwald. Both were used to foment rebellion and sabotage in the area. Nightly the appeal went out via the BBC Overseas Service, being broadcast every hour: 'POMALU PRACUJ. POMALU PRACUJ', 'WORK SLOWLY.'

This, despite threats and bribes, the local workers did – and more. To the horror of the German minority who ruled the Slav majority with an iron hand, they started to sabotage their own factories and communications. It wasn't difficult for the spymasters and string-pullers in London and Moscow to convince them to do so. The Czech workers were disgruntled. Their new German bosses treated them like third-class citizens and they didn't get the heavy workers' rations they knew German workers in the war industry received. What particularly rankled was that they received only part of their cigarette ration. In order to buy more, they had to resort to the flourishing black market, over which those same German bosses who kept them short held sway.

As a result the first strikes among Czech workers occurred and arsonists began their work. In August, 1941, 100,000 tons of fuel went up in flames. Telephone lines were cut, goods wagons sabotaged. By September, 1941, production in the Bohemian war industry had fallen by eighteen per cent; in some factories it went down by thirty-five per cent. Something had to be done.

It seems that Hitler himself selected Heydrich to take over Bohemia. German agents had reported that a general strike was being planned there for 28 October, 1941. Hitler knew that would have a disastrous effect on the Russian front. He knew, too, that it needed someone like the 'man with the iron heart', as he called Heydrich, to restore order. Yes, Reinhard Heydrich was the man. After an initial visit to Czechoslovakia, Heydrich for the first time, reported personally to the Führer on the conditions there. Hitler knew he would be stepping on the toes of important figures in both the Party and the German Diplomatic Corps by his action, but he went ahead and named Heydrich as the 'temporary *Reichsprotektor*'. At the age of 37 the man who had been mocked as an 'Izzy' in his youth, who had been cashiered from the German Navy, had become the effective leader of a country, albeit an enemy one, but still a country. That evening he informed his pregnant wife that he had been selected 'by the Führer to proceed to Prague to restore order there'.

His wife's reaction was to burst into tears. Later she would record, 'The news was terrible for me. He was never at home, or better, he was a visitor in our house. I'd been married to Reinhard Heydrich for ten years and in that time he must have spent seven years away.' She said to him, 'It would have been better if you'd have become a postman.'

But she couldn't dampen her husband's enthusiasm. 'Can't you understand what this means to me? Finally a really positive task. At last something better than being the trashcan of the nation.' But Lina wasn't convinced.

Three days after his arrival in Prague Heydrich summoned the local German leaders and told them, 'The Czechs have no role to play in the future of the New Europe. The racially valuable part of the Czech race will be germanized. As for the rest, they'll be "sterilized or put against the wall".' It was a harsh speech, in which there was no mention of a carrot for the Czech people, only the stick. Soon Heydrich would change his tactics and lay the foundations of the kind of Europe we now live in nearly sixty years later, astounding as it may seem. The 'New Europe' was a German concept that would reappear after Germany's defeat in 1945, albeit in a different guise. All the same, it would be German-run. But that would be long after Heydrich was dead.

Within a week Heydrich had set to work. Almost at once he

gained for himself the nickname of 'the Butcher of Prague', on account of his ruthless elimination of the Czech intelligentsia, stubborn politicians who wouldn't bend their will to that of the Germans and, naturally, Jews. But while his SS extermination *Kommandos* and SD agents were taking care of that problem, his civilian advisers were working on the problem of the Czech workers and the armament factories. This time they couldn't apply the measures which had worked so effectively in France, Belgium and the Low Countries, where they had promised the local labour bosses and factory owners no strikes and a secure profit. They couldn't, because in Bohemia *the bosses were German*!

Instead they started giving the Czech workers the same benefits that German workers enjoyed, albeit in a modified fashion. Immediately, the fat and cigarette rations were raised for heavy workers. Hotels in the plushier Bohemian resorts such as Karlsbad were requisitioned as holiday homes for Czech workers. Those who were run down were sent off on a paid *Kur* (cure) to spas where they could enjoy the waters and a discreet night life and be fussed over by doctors and nurses. For the first time in the history of the Czech Republic sick insurance and social security benefits on the German model were introduced.

The results were almost immediate. The Czech workers began to co-operate. They asked themselves why cut off their noses to spite their faces for the sake of those remote politicians, safe in London and Moscow. Production figures started to mount. The workers, fatter now, and with pockets full of cash, could start buying again. But not on the black market any more. For Heydrich had insisted on a crackdown. Black marketeers were arrested and charged, whether they were Czech or German, were shot and the details published in the local press. Even the ranking official in the Ministry of Agriculture, one Otokar Frankenberger, was executed for participating in a massive scam on the black market. Heydrich's 'soup economics' (*Suppenwirtschaft*), as he called the new measures, started to pay dividends.

Now the apostle of racial purity went one further. He

petitioned Berlin to allow Czechs to apply for German nationality. This was something unheard of. Even today it is a hot issue in democratic Germany. Anyone who can prove that he or she possesses one German grandparent can apply under the terms of the nineteenth century 'Blood Law' for German citizenship. On the other hand, Turks who have been in the country for three generations, whose children know only Germany and speak no other language than German, have a long and very difficult path ahead of them if they wish to become citizens of the country in which they were born. Although these Turks numbered almost a million in 1998, only a handful have succeeded in becoming German citizens. It is the same with the other nationalities who came to West Germany as 'guest workers' at the time of the 'Economic Miracle' in the 1950s. Germany's official policy on who can become a German remains as hard-nosed as it was in the days of the Kaiser.

But Heydrich maintained that anyone 'who builds a tank for the German Army ought to enjoy the pleasure of knowing that he does it for his *own* country'. This drastic and up-to-now unheard-of measure was approved and hundreds of Czechs with names such as Cihacek, Doskocil and Krzals were transformed into good German Forsters, Rotters and Schwarzs.

But Heydrich's success with his 'carrot and stick' technique was to be the foundation of his downfall. Although he was virtually unknown abroad, Czech Intelligence, or what was left of it in the country, had become conscious of this dangerous new force which was transforming their countrymen from resisters into collaborators.

Already Agent 'A-54' or 'Réné', to use another of his cover names, had fingered Heydrich as a man to be watched. Even before the *Gruppenführer* had been appointed to the Protectorate, Czech Intelligence's most important and most secret agent had been aware of the danger he would present if he were actually given the job in Prague. The fact that 'A-54' had known *in advance* that there was going to be a change at the top is not all that surprising. For 'A-54', perhaps the most important European agent on either side in the Second World War, had accepted the honour that Heydrich had once refused. He was, in fact, a long-time *Duzfreund** of no less a person than *Reichsführer SS* Heinrich Himmler, Heydrich's boss.

* The special German honour of addressing someone with the familiar 'thou'.

2

On the morning of 15 March, 1939, the readers of the London *Daily Mail* opened their newspaper to see the headline in inch-high letters declaring 'THREE ARMIES ON THE MARCH Germans, Hungarians and Retreating Czechs'. German and Hungarian troops had moved into the last part of independent Czechoslovakia and, apart from one Czech regiment which had stayed behind to fight, the rest of the Czech Army was in retreat.

Just below the main story there was a picture of three men peering out of an aircraft which had just landed at Croydon Airport with the caption, 'Eleven Mystery Men Arrive by Air, Sign Secret Register'. According to the journalist who had written the story, the eleven men who had arrived by KLM plane from Prague at 'ten o'clock last night' were 'believed to be members of the former Czech Government'. In fact they were the top members of the Czech Intelligence Service under the command of Lieutenant-Colonel Frantisek Moravec. The night before they had frantically looted their own Intelligence files, which were then shipped out of Prague under diplomatic seal, whereupon they had hurried to the waiting plane at Prague Airport. They did so in what they stood up in, not even telling their loved ones what they planned. As Moravec said after the war, 'I merely said I was going on an overnight trip to Moravia and asked my wife to pack a couple of shirts and some toothpaste.'

Now they were exiles in London, short of funds and friendless, for their former country had no agreement with Britain. But they had brought a priceless offering with them for their colleagues of the British Secret Intelligence Service–Agent 'A-54'.

'A-54', or Paul Thuemmel, was an ideally placed agent for the Czechs, since he had easy access to top German sources. Not only had he been a founder member of the National Socialist Party in his native Saxony and a *Duzfreund* of Himmler, but he was also a key agent in the German *Abwehr*, able to move across Occupied Europe without questions being asked. For some reason known only to himself Thuemmel had volunteered his services to the surprised Czechs back in the late '30s. Although initially suspicious, they had accepted him and found they had struck gold.

Thuemmel had warned them when their country would be invaded. He had given them the date of the attack on France and then, after the Czechs had begun working with the SIS, he told them that Operation Sealion had been postponed and that, instead, Hitler was intending to invade Russia.

Back in 1939, with the British Intelligence network in continental Europe vanishing so fast that in 1940 Churchill could declare, 'I can tell the time by the clock tower at Calais [he was speaking from Dover], but that's about all I know of affairs over there,' 'A-54' was the Czechs' card up the sleeve. The German traitor had opened the door to Whitehall for them, for he continued to supply the information that the planners desperately needed. Thus it was that the tiny and controversial Czech government in exile under Dr Benes wielded more influence in London than it warranted. While the SIS floundered, clutching at straws, the Czechs supplied the goods.

Heydrich didn't know this, but he *did* know from his own SD agents and those of Canaris' *Abwehr* – both outfits were spying on one another by now – that 'A-54' was in daily contact with London by radio. He guessed it was this particular spy who was sending the London Czechs the details of what was happening in their country, information which they used later in their anti-German propaganda broadcast by the BBC.

'A-54' had to be found and, with his usual dislike of delegating important tasks to other people, Heydrich took over the job of finding the unknown spy personally.

With Heydrich pushing, cajoling and threatening, things moved fast. 'A-54's code was broken by the SD radio specialists. 'Traitor X Group,' as Heydrich's special search group was known, followed up the leads given by the cracked intercepts. Eleven days after the agent's code was broken, he was trapped and captured. The real name and role of 'A-54', otherwise Paul Thuemmel, came as a great shock. How did one proceed against a long-time friend of the boss? In addition, Thuemmel had too many friends in high places to subject him to the kind of treatment that would have been meted out to a normal agent. Instead Heydrich was forced to use kid gloves. Thuemmel was confined to his quarters under a kind of open arrest, watched over by a single guard. Indeed his treatment was so lax that one evening when the guard was asleep he managed to sneak out and tell a Czech contact what had happened to him.

But now the old Gestapo hands took over. In postwar movies such people were always portrayed as brutal thugs who beat information out of their prisoners. In reality most of the Gestapo officials entrusted with the interrogation of suspected spies, agents and the like were ex-cops who had learned their trade in the solid, plodding world of police procedures the world over. They knew all about the psychology of the policeman vis-à-vis the suspect. They knew *they* were in a position of power from which they could spring a surprise on the prisoner whenever they liked, while the suspect could only react. They knew how to check and double-check his statements, so that in the end the prisoner either made a slip or confessed just to get some respite. Besides, any attempt to use 'sharp questioning', as torture was called in their procedural manuals, had to be referred in most cases to Himmler himself.

Thus, while Thuemmel was protected by the fact he was an intimate of Himmler so that no 'sharp questioning' could be used in his case, he stood little chance of getting away with his treachery when faced with a veteran like Willi Abendschoen.

Abendschoen had been questioning Stevens and Best when he was summoned by Gestapo Müller personally and sent to

Prague. Now he took his time, applying the old tried and trusted techniques. Over and over again Thuemmel, who thought he was still outwitting the policeman, went through the same old statement: where he had been when; who he had met; where he had stayed; what he had done in his off-duty time. Abendschoen listened patiently, occasionally applying the old 'sweet and sour' technique, but not often, on account of Thuemmel's position. At night he read and re-read Thuemmel's testimony looking for mistakes, incongruities. Then he thought he had it!

If Thuemmel had been working for Czech Intelligence, then he must have been in contact with the British too. After all, they had taken over the Czech Secret Servicemen when they fled into exile in London. Who would have benefited from Thuemmel's efforts save the British masters of the Czech snoopers? Had Thuemmel, then, had direct contact with the British?

Abendschoen remembered from his interrogation of Best and Stevens (who, in the end, had confessed enough to ruin their postwar reputation in the SIS) that they had said that in late 1939 a high-ranking German had come to visit the representative of Czech Intelligence at the British Embassy's Passport Office in The Hague*. Was this 'high-ranking German' Thuemmel, Abendschoen asked himself, or just another of those German traitors trying to make contact with the British Government. There had been a whole slew of them at the time.** The wary old cop tried to check. Within twenty-four hours he had struck gold. Checking through Thuemmel's personal records and expense account for 1939, Abendschoen discovered that on the dates in question Paul Thuemmel *had* been in the *Abwehr*'s Münster branch on his way to the Hague.

* Prior to 1939, the Passport Office in major British embassies had always been the base for the local SIS representative.
** Peter Ustinov, in his autobiography *Dear Me*, recounts how his father's flat at No 134, Redcliffe Gardens, London, S.W.10, was used for one such clandestine meeting between the SIS and German Major-General Geyr von Schweppenburg.

11. "Lina Heydrich loved Panenske Brezany" (p. 116).

12. "There is a photograph of the family in that final period of their life together" (p.116).

13. "Two young Czech patriots... were preparing to take their revenge" (p.57.)
Josef Gabick and Jan Kubis.

14. Mrs Ellison's daughter Edna holding Kubis's farewell note (right).
See p.99 et seq.

Text labels within the image:

JOSEF VACLIK
mit Signalspiegel
(a)

HEYDRICH
mit Chauffeur
(d)

JAN KUBIS
mit Handgranate
(b)

33

JOSEF GABCIK
mit Maschinenpistole
(c)

15. Lina Heydrich's sketch of the assassination: (a) Vaclik with mirror; (b) Kubis with hand grenade; (c) Gabcik with machine pistol; (d) Heydrich and driver (see p.145 et seq).

16. "The grenade hit the rear wheel and exploded" (p. 146).

17. Heydrich's funeral, Prague, June, 1942.

Thereafter it took some time to convict Thuemmel. Even Heydrich had to proceed with care and get Bormann's approval.* Secret arrangements were made at the highest level first to remove the prisoner from the National Socialist Party before anything further was done with him. Finally he was put in Theresienstadt Concentration Camp under the false name of Major Peter Tilman. He was supposedly a former Dutch military attaché, though he didn't speak a word of Dutch. And there he languished, for reasons known only to Himmler, Bormann and Heydrich, until he was shot in the spring of 1945.

But in a way the discovery of the Czech's most important agent and the network of spies, known as the 'Three Kings', which he had built up around him, had come too late. Week after week the 'Three Kings' Network' had passed on the statistics of the improved Bohemian *Drehscheibe* to London and they were the kind of figures that Dr Benes, could not tolerate. They questioned his very right to run the supposedly pro-allied government of a country which was clearly actively supporting the enemy. The writing was on the wall for Heydrich.

* Since Hitler had started to concentrate on the war in Russia, Bormann had begun to control the home front to an ever increasing degree.

3

Heydrich had no sense of the value of money. Once he told Lina that an applicant for a job with the SD had actually asked what the salary would be if he got the post. Heydrich thought that was 'scandalous'. He was no different in his private affairs. At times, he had been poor, especially after his dismissal from the *Kriegsmarine*, but that had not cured his extravagance, or rather, his lack of concern about money. Indeed, after Lina married him she was astonished to find that he possessed no less than thirty-odd old-fashioned naval dress shirts! She asked where they had all come from. He said that he had bought a new shirt every time an old one was dirty. Why hadn't he had them washed? 'Oh, I just took them off, threw them in the bath and hoped that someone would deal with them'.

Now, as 1941 gave way to 1942 and in faraway London the alarm bells were sounding, Heydrich was confronted for the very first time with the economics of the Empire he had built up.

Although the Eichmann group were already experimenting with gas – introducing it by means of the engine of a captured Russian submarine into the quarters used by some Jews and suffocating the inmates – there were hundreds of thousands of them costing the SS a fortune, until Eichmann again came up with a temporary solution. Why not make them produce goods for Germany's victory and at the same time pay back the various lending banks while they earned their own keep?

Heydrich and his cronies, who hitherto had been virtually totally responsible for dealing with the Jews, thought the idea brilliant. But how would the Jews be organized, categorized and allotted to work details? There simply weren't enough responsible German guards to do the job.

Eichmann, *der Judenexperte* as he liked to be called, who had studied the social structure and hierachy of Jewish communities, came up with a ready answer. It was to make certain Jews honorary members of the SS! In the course of his study, Eichmann had learned that for generations the orthodox Jews of the East had been governed by the *kehillah*, a kind of council of Jewish Elders. These were elected by the vote of their community to be a spokesman for their interests, protect them as best they could against the capricious nature of their gentile rulers and ensure that religious and social practices were carried out.

Now Eichmann and his subordinates approached these *Kehilloth* (the plural form in Hebrew) and asked them, though 'asked' probably wasn't exactly the way they did it, if they would help to set up what the Germans called *Judenräte* (Jewish councils). The latter would be used, so the SS-SD maintained, to run the great new ghettoes being established in Central Europe under Heydrich's command. We don't know how many of the *kehilloth* refused and what happened to those who did, but we *do* know that a large number did agree to help form these Jewish Councils from their own ranks.

So, as *Schindler's List*, the US movie, shows in detail, in ghettoes such as those in Cracow, Lublin and Warsaw, the Jews began to organize themselves, running a camp within a camp, with the German *Kapos* (usually communists) of the pre-war German concentration camps being replaced by Jewish policemen. Uniformed and armed with clubs, they kept order without the assistance of the SS guards, while the Jewish council selected those who were capable of work, work almost exclusively concerned with the German war machine. Those who were unfit, unskilled or unwilling were dealt with, not primarily by the Germans, but by the Council and their police force.

It is perhaps better to gloss over the details of these men and women who were prepared to sacrifice their fellow Jews rather than lose their own lives and who willingly helped the state which was liquidating their co-religionists. It is one of the darkest chapters of the history of the Second World War and is probably better left closed.

But in essence by this time Heydrich, wittingly or otherwise, had under his control a kind of rudimentary, but well-organized, Henry Ford 'assembly line' for Jews. It started with forced mass emigration; in the course of which they were stripped of their wealth and property. Bank accounts, shops, household goods – and for rich Jews the sums assessed were considerable – the proceeds from these all went into the coffers of the SS.

Thereafter came the work potential of the *Emigrant* – as they were often called by German officialdom. Were they capable of working or not? In the latter case they were disposed of – slowly by starvation, rapidly by execution. But even here the dead had some monetary value. Hair, gold teeth, gold-rimmed spectacles – one doesn't need to go through the whole gruesome litany; it is too well known – were all used to realize money for the SS.

Then finally came the camps, the ghettoes, the *Kommandos* and the other concentrations of forced Jewish labour. When the members of the *Judenrat* allotted Jews capable of working to their new employers the former were expected to keep tabs on them. Even though their employers were virtually all German, the SS expected to be paid for the labour provided by these 'slaves'. They might only earn a pittance, but the money went to finance the new empire that the SS had created.

But this new source of income caught the SS by surprise. Some of the money had to be paid to the big German banks, but those repayments didn't exhaust the SS's resources. What was to be done with the rest?

It was here that the collusion between the German banks and the SS began. Under the command of *SS Obergruppenführer* Oswald Pohl, an organization was set up to run the new economic side of the 'Black Guards'. Naturally the big banks, which traditionally have always promoted, openly or secretly, cartels and investment in industry, so that, even to this day, they basically control German industry, wanted to get into the act.*

They didn't just content themselves with building their own concentration camps near the sites of this cheap Jewish labour, but looked to the future and sought means of using their gains from Jewish industry to ensure that, whatever happened, the banks would function after the war was over. And they found an outlet for this money in a strange organization, which officially was run from neutral Switzerland, but which, in reality, was controlled not only from Berlin but also from London and New York!

After the First World War a special bank was set up in Basle in Switzerland. This was the Bank of International Settlements (BIS) and it was set up by the victorious Allies to ensure that the reparations imposed on the defeated Imperial Germany would be paid. On its board were representatives of key international financial institutions, the Bank of England, the First National Bank of New York, the Bank of Italy, the Bank of France and, naturally, the bank which was going to ensure that German payments were met, the *Reichsbank* situated in Berlin.**

The founders of the BIS made one important stipulation which was incorporated in its charter: the BIS could never be closed, seized or sanctioned, even if another war broke out between the directors' home nations. At the start of the Second World War with the bank still operating and the various directors from the warring nations still continuing to meet, its President was an American, Thomas McKittrick. Under him

* By putting their directors on the boards of large industrial companies, German banks effectively control the great German firms to this very day. They lend the firms the capital they need and then ensure, by means of these directors, that their money is spent in a manner with which they agree. It is a kind of financial relationship which is uncommon in the western democracies. Anglo-American anti-trust laws wouldn't allow it.
** The forerunner of Europe's currently most powerful bank (1998), *die Bundesbank*, the German Federal Bank.

he had a whole group of allied and enemy officials, plus two directors who would one day be classified as war criminals: the head of the *Reichsbank*, Emil Puhl, and its vice-president, Walter Funk.

Naturally the British knew who these Germans were, but when Churchill queried the role of Funk and Puhl, he was appeased by the Chancellor of the Exchequer and the Governor of the Bank of England.* They said the Germans were not taking advantage of Britain's continental interests, but that was not true.

In fact the BIS was used, along with the Swiss banks, as a conduit for the Nazi gold and assets that Heydrich's new economic empire had realized. But it was to go further than that. As one Swiss historian, Gian Trepp, who has studied the whole business, still even now wrapped in secrecy (especially since the Swiss finance world has been rocked by the 'Nazi Gold' revelations by US Senator d'Amato) has written: 'Even during the war the moneymen of different nations needed to keep in touch, because when the war stops you have to rebuild and you need free trade.'

In other words German big business was, via the banks, running the BIS, thus hedging its bets. It was preparing for the 'worst scenario' – the defeat of Nazi Germany. While McKittrick rubbed shoulders with Puhl over drinks in Basle and Zurich, Heydrich's Jews provided the capital which might well one day be used to rebuild a Fourth Reich, whatever form that might take.** Already there was one maverick SD officer

---

* Even a half a century later, when the author made enquiries about the role of the wartime Governor of the Bank of England, Sir Montagu Norman, who definitely had links with Nazi bankers in the early years of the war, the Bank refused to reveal details. Indeed, even Churchill at that time could not get information on Norman, whom he suspected of co-operation with the Germans.
** Amazingly enough, the Bank of England was empowered by Chamberlain, when he was Prime Minister, to allow the German conquerors to receive back the Czech gold reserves which had been taken out of that country with British help. Chamberlain, when questioned about that matter, stood up in Parliament on 16 May, 1939, and answered the question, 'Is it true that the national treasure of Czechoslovakia is being given to Germany?' with, 'It is not.' It was a blatant lie and the PM knew it.

making plans, even when it seemed that Germany was all-conquering, for that possibility. He was *Obergruppenführer* Otto Ohlendorf, head of Internal Security in the Heydrich Empire, an SD officer who, between 1941 and 1942, had been responsible for the murder of 90,000 Soviet citizens in the Crimea. This was the man, hanged at Nuremberg, who would unwittingly start the chain of events which would lead to the creation of the German 'Free Market Economy' of the post-war Federal Republic – and to the Common Market.

4

Otto Ohlendorf, who had joined the SS in the mid-thirties, was one of the most controversial characters in the whole bizarre world of the SS. Hitler's 'Black Guards' was full of crackpots, but none of them present such a puzzle as Ohlendorf. In Russia he commanded one of the extermination commandos which put to death thousands of innocent civilians, yet at the same time he was appalled by the crudity and greed of his fellow SS officers and was prepared to use his position to clean up the organization and prosecute those who broke its laws.

Unfortunately for the SS, and in particular Himmler, who needed him but didn't like him one bit, after Russia Ohlendorf had been given the SD's strangely named 'Spheres of Life' Office. Part of his job was to vet reports from agents all over the Reich, the so-called *Meldungen aus dem Reich* (Reports from the Reich). These were issued to top Party members two or three times a week and informed them of the man-in-the-street's comments on Party bosses' greed, arrogance and general wrongdoings. Naturally Himmler was a recipient of these messages of gloom and doom and naturally he didn't like them, feeling that they were calculated to harm the reputation of the Party and, in particular, the SS.

In 1942 Himmler was receiving complaints about the reports every week through Bormann from other Party bosses, but he encouraged Ohlendorf, who was, as Himmler knew, an honest man, to occupy himself with other fields that came within the scope of his office.

Ohlendorf seems to have taken the *Reichsführer* at his word, for, as the money from Heydrich's camps came flooding in by the million and the German industries, which co-operated with Heydrich and profited from his Eastern 'enterprises', started to wonder what the future would hold for them, Ohlendorf turned his attention to the war economy in general and to Heydrich's assets in particular.

He was an educated man who understood something of macro-economics. Indeed, almost as soon as he joined the SS he warned that one of the two great dangers threatening the life of the Party would be 'collective tendencies in economic and social policy'. And it was 'collective tendencies' in economic affairs that the bankers who supported Heydrich hated like the devil. After all, those same collective economic tendencies in Soviet Russia had totally destroyed the independent banking sector.

Now, at the turn of 1941/42, with Germany at the height of its power, Ohlendorf turned to a secretive group called *Reichsgruppe-Industrie* (roughly the Reich Industrial Group). This was made up of representatives of Germany's top firms, including IG Farben, the Deutsche and Dresdner Banks, Reemtsma and the greatest of them all, Flick,* indeed all the firms, or their forebears, which would create postwar Germany.

Within the framework of the Office of Spheres of Life, this group of industrial giants set up a research foundation, the *Institut für Industrieforschung* (Institute for Industrial Research). This institute was now going to think the unthinkable: *how should German industry be reorganized after defeat?*

The man who was given the task of heading the institute was a roly-poly German university teacher from Southern Germany, given to good wine and big cigars, but whose ruddy face looked like 'a plump baby's bottom', it was so unwrinkled. The fat professor was a good German. He had shed his blood

* In 1997 Oxford University turned down a very large donation by the Flick grandson, who lives in London. The full reasons weren't given at the time, but any Oxford economist worth his salt must have known why.

for Germany in the First World War and had nearly lost an arm at Ypres in 1918. All the same he had little time for the Nazis, which had meant his academic career had come to a virtual standstill. But he refused to join the Party. Now, in 1942, his brother-in-law, Karl Guth, the manager of *Reichsgruppe-Industrie*, offered him the Institute for Industrial Research and with it the secret research project already mentioned. Why he took it is not known now. If Heydrich, his indirect boss, had ever found out, he would undoubtedly have been sent to one of the camps as a traitor. But he never did.

So for the next two years the Professor laboured on his research paper. In March, 1944, he produced his results.*. This paper and its gloomy statistics were eventually seen by Ohlendorf who then had a long discussion with the Professor in total privacy or 'under four eyes', as the Germans put it. The result was that Ohlendorf empowered him to continue his research, while the great industrialists set about making their own preparations for peace and ensuring their future. Naturally they used their old friends in Switzerland and their new ones in France, Belgium, Holland and Luxembourg, the same friends who would be the founding members of the Common Market.

The details of these discussions, held, significantly enough, in Strasbourg, one of the three bases of today's EEC, are still not known and probably never will be. But one thing is certain. The Professor continued with his research until, in January, 1945, he met a young recruit to Ohlendorf's organization, Karl Guenther Weiss. The Professor told him that he wanted somehow to disassociate himself from the SS and its *Weltanschauung*, but he couldn't think of a better name for his new economic theories. According to Weiss, he suggested 'Social Market Economy', which he thought was a name that Ohlendorf would accept. The Professor said, 'I like that name. If you'd like another glass of Burgundy, we'll drink a toast to it.'**

It was midday on 12 January, 1945. Professor Ludwig Erhard,

* *War Finance and Consolidation of Debts*
** Karl Guenther Weiss, *Wahrheit und Wirklichkeit*, 1996.

94

one day to be an economics adviser to the US military govern-
ment and, much more importantly, Western Germany's second
Chancellor, had just celebrated the theory which would create
Germany's 'economic miracle'.

Outside the war still raged. In the Ardennes the Allies were
fighting to regain the territory they had lost in the German
surprise offensive of December, 1944. In East Prussia and
Poland the Russians, taking advantage of the fact that currently
the main Nazi effort was being employed in the West, had
begun their last great offensive which would take them to the
gates of Berlin. In the camps, now totally disorganized and
virtually out of control, with disease raging and starvation
everywhere, hundreds of thousands of inmates succumbed.

The Germans had committed bestial crimes the like of which
Europe had not seen since the Thirty Years War of the early
seventeenth century, whole populations being ruthlessly
wiped out. Her cities were in ruins, shattered by years of Allied
bombing. Her casualties had been tremendous at least three
million civilians had been killed in the previous five years.
What could the future hold for this outcast among nations?
None, the perceptive observer of the time who knew the facts
might have opined. Yet within five years that totally discredited country was back on its feet again. Five more and it had
become the leading economic power in Europe, far outpacing
the supposed victors, Britain and France. How was it possible?

As we have seen, the answer lay in the country's wartime
past. But Heydrich would never see that new Germany. He was
murdered long before it came into being, ironically enough
because, for once, he had done some good for his fellow human
beings, the Czech workers.

But the venal businessmen who were profiting from
Heydrich's crimes in 1942 would survive. Just as they had been
honoured by the Third Reich, they would be so once again in
that postwar Germany of the 'economic miracle' and the 'hard
D-Mark'. They would die peacefully in their beds, old and
respected.

V

AN ASSASSINATION IS PLANNED

'They speak of murder . . . I can't trust anyone any more. Assassination awaits me on the least suspicion'.

Felix Stidger, US Union Spy, 1864.

1

In Britain 1942 was the period of the war which those who were alive at the time cared least to look back on later. Yet, to all intents and purposes the mass German bombing had ceased and, thanks to Ultra and other measures, the U-boat blockade of the British Isles would soon come to an end. Already rations had started to improve slightly. People could even enjoy the old working-class standby once more: the fish shops were serving fish again to go with the chips!

All the same it seemed to the survivors that this was a grey time in the greyest period of a long grey war. Admittedly the sun shone early that year; in fact it would be the hottest summer of the war. But the people seemed fagged out. There had been one defeat after another since the BEF had been kicked out of France in June, 1940, and even Churchill, who had rallied the nation thereafter, could not seem to promise anything better in the near future. SECOND FRONT NOW, the communist-inspired slogan, adorned walls and bridges everywhere. But everyone knew that was just a pious hope. There'd be no attack across the Channel this year, and probably not the next either.

Meanwhile the long-suffering civilians tried to take their minds off the war. They went to the pictures. They went to the pubs and fought to get a warm, weak glass of beer before the landlord announced, 'No more ale, ladies and gents. We've run out.' They went to the *palais de danse* and swirled around in the dances of the time, even if most of the 'squaddies' wore hob-nailed boots. Or they simply 'went out'.

Mrs Ellison's two daughters, fifteen and sixteen, were too young for such pleasures. Besides they were village girls from Ightfield, Cheshire, and were wary of the temptations of the surrounding towns. Everyone knew the shame a girl would bring on her family if she weren't married and 'got caught'. There were plenty of young men in uniform out at night, and they weren't all British. There were Poles, French, Belgians and now, in their own area, Czechs. Mrs Ellison knew little of Czechoslovakia. She would have been hard put to it to identify it on a map. But she did know that the Czechs were as dangerous as any of the other foreigners. They were *men* after all! So it came as a shock to her when her daughters came home from an afternoon in Whitchurch buzzing with excitement. They had been picked up! They had been waiting for the old single-decker bus to take them back to their village when a handsome young Czech soldier had tried to talk to them. Their giggles at his strange English had given him pause, but just as the bus was about to set off he'd passed a note through the window. It had read in a pencilled scrawl: 'Please meet me here tomorrow.'

Mrs Ellison, as she recalled years later, 'soon put the moppers on that'. No daughters of hers would be meeting a man just like that, especially a stranger in a foreign uniform, here today and gone tomorrow. God only knew what the consequences might be. The two girls were forbidden to meet this unknown Czech.

But for a while fate was on his side. A week later Mrs Ellison had been in Whitchurch with the two girls when there he was again. He stopped immediately and saluted – something that Mrs Ellison had never experienced before. Then, in his fractured English, he tried to make a polite conversation. For a few minutes the mother was in a quandary. What was she to do? Then her good heart got the better of her. He seemed a nice, lonely young man. On impulse she invited him to come with them to the pictures and followed that invitation with another. Warning him that the last bus from Ightfield left early and he might have to walk back to camp, she invited him to tea. He accepted with alacrity and before he left Mrs Ellison extended an open invitation to him, saying, 'Come and see us on your days off. If you like you can come and stay here if you get a leave.' The war had broken down her traditional British reticence and she didn't feel too bad about making the offer. His high-cheekboned Slavic face lit up. As best he could in English, he stammered that he'd like it 'ver-ry much'. The relationship had been established. Josef Gabcik had appeared on the scene.

Over the months that followed Josef became a regular visitor to the little red-brick house. As a young man he must have had a sexual appetite. To whom it was directed we don't know, but he got on well with the mother and with the girls, Lorna and Edna. His English improved, but sometimes he seemed to be in another world, so remote that Mrs Ellison felt constrained to wake him from his reverie.

But underneath his introspection there lay a volatile temper. As the Ellisons recalled when they learned the real nature of their guest: 'If Josef missed a bus or knocked a drink over up he soared like a rocket, spurting rage. Then he would laugh himself down to ground level again.'

In a way that temperament was ideal for the violent business that lay ahead; at the same time it could lead to difficulties. Fortunately, however, Gabcik introduced another Czech to the Ellison household who was to be his comrade in the events to come and he was of a totally different temperament.

In 1941 Jan Kubis was twenty-eight. The son of a peasant, he had served as a sergeant in the Czech Army before taking the same route as his comrade through Poland into the Foreign Legion – the Czech Division, with which he had won the Czech War Cross in the fighting in France – before allowing himself to be evacuated to Britain hoping to continue the war against Germany from there in the ranks of the Czech Brigade. But the months had passed without any sign of action and in the end he had decided to join the Czechs in the RAF who had already been in action during the Battle of Britain. He had written on his application for a transfer: 'I should be glad if I could carry out the duties of a gunner. For all these reasons

I beg you to give my request a favourable reception'. He would never become an RAF air gunner, but he did achieve his aim of getting back into action, perhaps sooner than he had anticipated, and the manner of his death in action against the Germans would make him a Czech national hero for all times.

So the months passed with Mrs Ellison, in her own quiet way, studying her 'two boys' and wondering what would happen to them when, one day, they would go, as they surely would. There was something, however, which perplexed and worried her. When they shared her back bedroom they laid a wicker-work basket beneath the window. It was something they did naturally, as if it was the most obvious thing in the world. Then, before they turned in for the night, they put in the basket two cumbersome British Army service revolvers. To them it clearly didn't seem a strange thing to do. To Mrs Ellison it did. England was at war admittedly, but nothing dangerous ever happened in this remote place. So why did these two young men prepare to fight every night before they went to sleep? What were they really up to?

Both of them had good reason to be always on their guard, even here in friendly rural England. For years they had been prepared for the worst, the sudden knock on the door, the stamp of heavy boots, harsh German voices that always sounded as if they were barking out a command even when they weren't. It seemed to be part and parcel of the language of their oppressors.

Several times in the last three or four years they had escaped by the skin of their teeth. Once Jan had been too slow and had survived only by the boldness of his friends who had rescued him from his cell and sent him on his way to cross yet another of the many borders he would cross illegally in the course of his short life.

Naturally a man who had swastikas branded on his bare buttocks by his torturers was always on his guard. But Jan was something else – he was a hater as well, a man consumed by an almost pathological desire for revenge on his torturers, who would go to virtually any length to exact it.

102

And the spymaster in London knew it. Patriotism was not enough. You had to hate with the fervour of a religion to do what he planned for these young men. Gabcik and Kubis carried revolvers because they knew they were always at risk.

2

In the autumn of 1941, while Kubis and Gabcik waited for their orders, President Benes of the Czech government in exile was a troubled man. He was worried by the attitude of the British Government, by whether the still neutral President Roosevelt would recognize his government and, naturally, what the Germans would do next in his own country.

Some said that he was dominated by a 'Munich Complex', that his country might be sacrificed again, as it had been by the Anglo-French in 1938, to some new agreement. A compromise peace with Germany or some sort of deal between Britain and Soviet Russia, now Britain's ally, might well mean the end of his government in favour of a new Czech government in exile, based perhaps in Moscow. That autumn anything seemed possible in view of the constant defeats suffered by both Britain and Russia.

It was for these reasons that Dr Benes conferred virtually every day with his Chief-of-Intelligence, Colonel Moravec, one of those eleven Czechs mentioned earlier who had landed at Croydon. Some wags joked that Moravec was the 'Czech Himmler', but Benes always maintained that he needed to see Moravec so frequently, and always alone, because 'politics needs intelligence and without it nothing gets done'.

But the real reason was that Moravec was the only really effective link he had to the British through the latter's working contacts with the SIS, and Benes knew only too well that the pragmatic British really assessed these many exile governments in London, which they were financing, by the effectiveness of their country's resistance to the Germans. In the first two years of the war this had been considerable. Agent 'A-54' had been one of the Czech aces, highly prized by British Intelligence and the British Government. Czech resistance and their sabotaging of the German war industry had also heightened his standing. But now, Heydrich having taken over with the resultant increase in war production in Bohemia the British had turned against him. By the autumn of 1941, Benes' government in exile ranked at the very bottom of the pecking order in London, even lower than that of Belgium, and Benes feared for his future. Something had to be done to restore Churchill's, and Roosevelt's, faith in the Czechs. But what?

It was obvious that whatever they did would have to originate in Britain. Czech resistance in the homeland had come to a virtual standstill. Its members had retreated to what they called 'diving stations'. Heydrich's punitive measures, especially the slaughter of student strikers in Prague a few weeks before – their bodies had been left on the pavements for all to see – had had their effect. The working classes had responded to his 'stick and carrot' treatment. Improved rations and working conditions had done the trick. Large-scale sabotage from within was definitely out of the question now.

So Benes would have to start with such resources as he possessed in Britain. With a bit of luck these measures would then be aided by what was left of the local underground. They hadn't the resources within Britain to carry out large-scale sabotage operations. The distances were too great, they didn't have enough trained men and no planes capable of reaching their homeland, still out of range of the RAF's bombers. Indeed Benes had already asked the RAF High Command to bomb the Czech war factories, although such bombing would mean the certain death of Czech workers. But the RAF had refused. They would have to fly over German-held territory most of the way and, with the payload in bombs and fuel their bombers would have to carry, they were not sure that their Wellington and Halifax aircraft would be able to make it back to base.

Benes and Moravec soon decided that some high-ranking German official would have to be assassinated. Naturally a successful assassination would engender German reprisals, which, in their turn, would occasion counter-measures on the part of the Czech underground. The cosy 'honeymoon' between the German victors and the Czech vanquished would soon come to an end and they would have achieved their aim. Apparently the cost in Czech lives never entered their calculations. If it did, we do not know, as we know so tantalizingly little about the whole operation. For, although the plotters worked out of London, presumably under observation of the SIS, MI5 and other agencies,* the latter seem to have kept no record of the Czechs' preparation for the murder to come. Indeed the one person from that period who should have known what the Czechs were proposing denies all these years later that he ever knew anything about the business. He was Churchill's coordinator of British Intelligence, Lord William Bentinck.

He stated flatly, when queried about the matter, that 'The JIC was never asked to approve the assassination of Heydrich in 1941 and I know nothing about this plan (if such a plan did exist), nor of the exile Czech opposition, but I can well imagine that the Czech government in exile would have objected, knowing the retribution that would follow this assassination.'**

But such matters did not apparently concern the two plotters. They knew from their own sources in what was left of the Czech underground that the Russians had already dropped para-sabotage teams intended for Czechoslovakia. They didn't have planes of sufficient range, so the agents had been dropped in Poland and told to make their way there by whatever means they could. On 10 September, 1941, they had been followed by another group of Czech communist

* In particular, both the Dutch and French Intelligence agencies in exile were watched by the British for leaks to the Germans, which there certainly were. Indeed the highest-ranking Dutchman in London, of royal blood at that, was definitely suspect. As General Stewart Menzies, head of the SIS, told the author's informant, 'Menzies snapped at me once, "Don't let that bloody Dutchman in to the HQ ever again. He's always sniffing around. Too much, if you ask me".'
** In a letter to the author.

21 CARLYLE SQUARE
LONDON S W 3
01-352-1258
OFFICE: 01-940-6077

Dear Mr. Whiting,

     I am writing in reply to your letter of December 13
in which you put three questions, my replies to these are:

1.   I think it is correct that the JIC was set up on
the basis of Lord Hankey's proposals for the re-
organisation of the Intelligence Services prior
to World War 2.

2.   I have no knowledge about the opposition to
Menzies's appointment; it is quite probable that
Admiral Godfrey opposed this appointment, but I
never heard that either Buck de la Warr or Gladwyn
Jebb were in any way opposed to this.

3.   The JIC was never asked to approve the assassination
of Heydrich in 1941 and I know nothing about this
plan (if such a plan did exist), nor of the exile
Czech opposition but I can well imagine that the
Czech government in exile would have objected
knowing the retribution that would follow this
assassination.

       Yours sincerely,

       W. Cavendish Bentinck

      Lord William Bentinck

agents who had established radio contact with their Soviet spy-masters.

This news, it can be imagined, lent haste to Benes' and Moravec's deliberations. Not only were they losing their influence in London, due to the arrest of 'A-54' and to Heydrich's efforts to appease the Czech workforce, but now the Soviets were in the game and establishing contact with the very strong communist underground. Churchill had already signed his 'pact with the Devil', as he called his agreement with Russia. Would he now agree to let Czechoslovakia slip into the Soviet sphere of influence? If he did, then the Czech government in exile in London was finished.

The *Reichsprotektor*, who by now Benes and Moravec had picked as the victim, had to be dealt with, and dealt with *soon*.

3

Back in the summer of 1940 Churchill had found himself in a quandary. The British had been thrown out of Europe and with the troops had fled the last of the SIS's and Military Intelligence's agent networks. He was eyeless in Gaza, and the PM didn't like it one bit. Nor did he care for the 'island mentality' which, he knew, would soon develop, with Britain left alone to face up to the Germans. Invariably such a situation would lead to a defensive mentality.

As early as 4 June, 1940, he minuted General Hastings Ismay, his military adviser: 'The completely defensive habit of mind which has ruined France must not be allowed to ruin our initiative. . . . How wonderful it would be if the Germans could be made to wonder where they were going to be struck next, instead of forcing us to try to wall in the Island and roof it over.'

Two days later he followed this with an urgent appeal to Ismay, asking: 'What arrangements are being made for good agents in Denmark, Holland, Belgium and along the French coast?' He wanted, he added, to see 'enterprises prepared with specially trained men . . . who can develop a reign of terror, so that the lives of German troops in occupied Europe be made an intense torment'.

Three weeks later, under the leadership of Lord Halifax, who had been behind the secret negotiations with the Germans the year before, plans were being drawn up for a new secret organization, which would eventually rival the discredited SIS, the Special Operations Executive (SOE) which would

109

'co-ordinate all subversive and sabotage actions against the enemy'.

The task of setting up this organization was given to Dr Hugh Dalton, the Labour Minister of Economic Warfare and now head of that organization which Churchill nicknamed approvingly 'the Ministry of Ungentlemanly Warfare'. Its task was, as the PM put it in his customary rousing terms, 'to set Europe ablaze'.

Naturally, by 1941 there was a Czech section in this new organization, but on the whole Benes and Moravec preferred to run their own agents. But they did use the SOE training schools all over Britain to train their spies, especially in learning how to parachute.

About 120 Czech agents had already been trained when Moravec had Gabcik and Kubis sent to learn these clandestine techniques. But although the finished products of these training schools appeared to be under British control when they were sent to 'STS 2', otherwise the Villa Bellasis, a requisitioned country house near Dorking, in fact they came under one of Colonel Moravec's officers. For 'STS 2', while manned by British personnel, was run by Captain Sustr of Czech Intelligence, who prepared the 'Joes', as they were known by their British instructors, for their specific operational tasks. Here the SOE exercised no control.

One of the Czech Intelligence instructors' main weaknesses, as the British saw it, was that they had no means of getting their agents out of Czechoslovakia once they had carried out their assignments. The agents would have to remain on the run, depending on the Czech underground for succour until they were either killed or their homeland liberated.

But, viewed from our own perspective, this was yet another advantage enjoyed by Benes and Moravec. They had selected the intended victim without recourse to the British. As we have seen from Bentinck's letter, the Joint Intelligence Committee, which was supposed to review and approve all such matters, was not in the picture. This meant, in theory at least, that Churchill did not know that the Czech government in exile intended to assassinate Heydrich. Nor could they learn from 'STS 2' what the Czechs were about. On the face of it the tail was wagging the dog. The Czechs were preparing an action which would certainly have important repercussions which even they could not foretell, and Churchill, who liked to have his finger in every pie, knew nothing about it. *

The Czech plotters' major concern was where they were going to find a plane to carry the would-be assassins. They couldn't call upon whatever warplanes were currently being flown by Czech pilots because all such planes were under the direct command of the RAF and RAF High Command was very reluctant to use its precious long-range bombers for dropping agents, and anyway the skilled crew needed for an operation of this kind were hard to come by. Bomb aimers in the RAF were still routinely dropping their cargo of sudden death up to *five miles* off their target and good navigators were few and far between. Hence, the order to allot a plane to a long-range parachute operation, in which there was a good chance that it might not return, had to come from the highest authority.

Churchill seems to have been out of the question. As we have seen, he had set his face against political assassination. Indeed, as it turned out, Heydrich would be the *only* prominent Nazi leader to be assassinated during the whole of the Second World War. A couple of *Gauleiters*, minor Nazi leaders in reality, were murdered, but in both cases the assassinations were carried out by partisan or similar organizations. So it would appear that Churchill did not give his sanction to the coming assassination; hence the fact that Bentinck denied that the case ever came up before the Joint Intelligence Committee. Churchill, invariably curious about Intelligence matters, was always kept informed of the JIC's important decisions.

* There seems to have been an unspoken agreement between Hitler and Churchill that there should be no attempt on either side to murder any of the leaders, German or British. It was only later in the war, after 1943, that various assassination attempts were made.

In later years there were claims that 'International Jewry' were involved. They wanted Heydrich killed before he presented his case for the extermination of all European Jews at the notorious 'Wannsee Conference' where the 'final solution' was decided upon. But who were these 'International Jews' and how did they exercise such power that they could obtain an RAF plane for the Czech assassins? How, indeed, did they know about the 'final solution' in advance when it has been only in recent years that Jewish researchers have discovered that details of what was really going on in the concentration camps only started to filter out in mid-1942. I think we can discount that possibility.

Naturally we can't underestimate the power of the SIS, especially when it had the backing of the British royal family. For it has been suggested that Heydrich, as Schellenberg's boss and Himmler's second-in-command, knew too much about the treasonable activities of the Duke of Windsor and his wife back in 1940 and it was for that reason that he was assassinated!

Hitler and Himmler had a kind of love-hate relationship with the British. They admired the British for their Empire, traditions and loyalty to their royal family, while hating them for not finishing the war in 1940 and letting the 'New Germany' get on with its self-imposed task of cleaning up Europe. But neither would ever have approved of the betrayal of the Duke of Windsor's confidences.

Heydrich certainly would. If it had served his and Germany's advantage, he wouldn't have hesitated to reveal all he knew about the Duke, and it was well known that he recorded any 'dirt' he acquired about his superiors. If he *did* possess anything incriminating on the Duke, Heydrich would have been a likely candidate for assassination by the British Establishment.

So what organization with the power to obtain an aircraft, no questions asked, is left? The answer is Dr Hugh Dalton's newly formed SOE, that hated rival of the long-established Secret Intelligence Service which, it appears, did not hesitate even at betrayal of its supposed comrades-in-arms in order to achieve ascendancy in countries which the SIS believed belonged to it exclusively. *

But would Dr Dalton, a Labour Minister in the Coalition Government, court political disaster by authorizing the use of an RAF plane for these assassins? Probably not. So that leaves two senior SOE figures below Dalton who might fit the bill: Sir Geoffrey Vickers VC, SOE's representative on the JIC, and Colonel Colin Gubbins. If we accept Bentinck's statement that the plan was never put to the Joint Intelligence Committee, that leaves the redoubtable Colin Gubbins.

When Gubbins arrived at SOE Headquarters he was a forty-five-year-old colonel. According to one SOE agent who knew him at the time, 'He looked one straight in the eye and spoke in short staccato sentences. A casual observer might have described him as a typical British colonel.' But his manner and bearing were deceptively orthodox. He might once have been a typical regular soldier, but his horizon was much larger than was usual in the breed. He was highly intelligent, widely read, and his gift of leadership was tempered by a generous sense of humour. It was something he was going to need in order to deal with the patriots, renegades, absent-minded professors, crack-pots and empire-builders he encountered in the ranks of this new hush-hush organization recruited from a dozen different nations.

All of them in due course found out two things about the Colonel. He was a difficult man to serve under. His rigid standards of integrity were not those of many of his subordinates, many of them politicians who had lived by comprise throughout their careers. He also wanted action, not a year hence, but *now*.

Gubbins had certain fixed ideas on what these foreign agents should do. One of them was that they should not foment a mass uprising of their native underground organizations until the Allies (basically Britain and, later, America) invaded their countries. Only then did he want mass dislocation of transport

* There is a good case for this assumption in the SOE/SIS rivalry in Holland during 1941/43.

and other services by the resistance put into effect. So in the case of the Czechs, who would probably be 'liberated' by the Russians anyway, the murder of one Nazi wouldn't disrupt his longterm plans. In theory he would have had no serious objection to the murder of Heydrich.

In any case it would come under the terms of Dalton's brief. As he had written to Lord Halifax back in 1940, 'We must organize movements in enemy-occupied territory comparable to the Sinn Fein in Ireland. . . . We must use many different methods, including industrial and military sabotage, labour agitation and strikes, continuous propaganda, terrorist acts against traitors and German leaders.' No wonder Churchill called the new organization 'the Ministry of Ungentlemanly Warfare'.

Dalton did apparently advocate 'terrorist acts' – which could only mean the assassination of Nazi Leaders. So was it he who approved the SOE scheme and helped the Czechs to obtain the aeroplane? Why should he have run the risk of having his proposals turned down by the Intelligence establishment, ie the SIS, which dominated the JIC and hated the SOE?

Did Dalton help not for the sake of the Czechs but because he wanted to help the Russians? Was he, like so many socialists of that time, with the honourable exception of Ernest Bevin, eager to do all he could for the hard-pressed Stalin? He knew that any disruption of the German-Czech industrial complex in Bohemia and of the Czech railway system, which played a vital role in the war in the East, would be a tremendous boost for the Russians. Not only would the assassination of Heydrich lead to reprisals among the Czech labour force, but it would also certainly destroy what was left of the Benes-led resistance.

Who then would continue the underground fight against the Germans until the Allies eventually took over? Obviously the existing communist resistance movement, already linked to Moscow by the score of agents parachuted in via Poland. And which ally would march in once victory had been achieved? Obviously Soviet Russia.

All this, however, is conjecture. All we know is that Dalton was the first to make the initial appeal to the RAF for one of their new Halifax four-engine bombers to fly in a group of Czech paras to their native country, and it appears that he made the appeal without the knowledge of the JIC. But in the end he was turned down by the RAF's High Command, so once again the ball was back in Benes' court.

4

Let us now glance at the family life of the Heydrichs in Czechoslovakia.

Officially their residence was the Hradcany, Prague's splendid palace-cum-castle. But Lina longed for a simpler home, in a rural setting in which she could bring up her children. In the end they took over a large country house outside Prague, and soon settled down there.

Lina loved Panenske Brezany, which was to be her home for the next four years. She tamed the Czech servants, even the squad of SS guards, which Himmler had personally assigned to the residence. Heydrich himself always travelled without guards, but he didn't object to these SS men, who he knew were 'pushing a quiet ball', as the Army phrase had it.* He had to ensure that his wife and children were protected against possible Czech attack. Not that he thought that was likely, as he was sure that he had broken the back of the Czech resistance.

There is a photo of the family (see plate 12) in that final period of their life together. Reinhard and Lina are dressed in their conception of a Bavarian *Tracht* outfit, she in a skirt and flowered top with white knee-high socks, he in black shorts with a grey woollen jacket with brass buttons, and white socks too. With them, on the lawn, is their newborn daughter Silke. They look happy, especially Lina. For once, presumably, she

* *'Eine ruhige Kugel schieben'*, a cushy number in British Army parlance.

116

can spend a whole day with Reinhard. For his part, he smiles coldly at the camera and, even though he looks relaxed, his eyes are as alert and wary as ever. He looks almost as if he is assessing the reliability of the photographer to take a good shot of them. But what is really going on behind that look?

We know from his wife that Heydrich felt he had created 'an oasis of peace' here in the midst of war. As she noted afterwards, 'Here is a world in which no fathers and sons die in battle. The only problem they [the Czechs] face here is being conscripted into the war industry where they earn more than the soldiers at the front, who, in the final analysis, have also to sacrifice their lives for their Fatherland.'

Yet as he played with his new child on the lawn that day nearly sixty years ago, he could never have dreamed that, in his way, he was creating a 'New Europe', one which now dominates all our lives. For while he took a few hours off from the war, his agents were still coining that money which, in a strange and indirect manner, would bring about the 'European Economic Community'.

Heydrich had recently been instrumental in having a German technocrat assigned to the Czech cabinet. Walter Bertsch was the new 'Czech' Minister of Labour, but, because he couldn't speak Czech, all cabinet discussions were now carried on in German. Currently Bertsch was presiding over a vast reorganization of Czech industry, which, prior to the Occupation, had been the leading economy in Eastern Europe. He shut all companies which weren't contributing to the war economy and a kind of industrial conscription was introduced. Workers weren't asked where they wanted to go after being declared redundant from 'unsuitable' jobs; they were *directed* on pain of imprisonment. By these means 100,000 workers were released and another 79,000 sent to work in the Reich's war industries.

A new shift system was to follow. Instead of three eight-hour shifts, the day was now split into two twelve-hour ones, which could be organized more profitably and efficiently. Profits started to rise and the SS, with an eye to the future, were vitally interested in profit.

Already Czech-owned pharmaceutical, wood-working and

leather industries were making a handsome profit. Now in an attempt to beat Field Marshal Goering at his own game,[*] Himmler decided that all the weapons production of the Skoda factories would be diverted to the *Waffen SS*. Indeed he wanted the director-general of the *Skoda-Werke*, a German with the honorary rank of *SS Standartenführer*, to produce a new series of light automatic weapons exclusively for the 'Armed SS'.

But while Himmler enjoyed the power, the prestige and the profits that came from this exclusive economic empire, Benes' problems also grew apace. It was clear by now that Bohemia was a major supplier of weapons to the Germans fighting on the Russian front. In addition, the puppet Slovakian government was now sending troops to fight in Russia. Whatever else he was, Benes was a realist. He knew that people were beginning to regard the Czechs as quislings, especially as the Czech puppet government, under the ageing Emil Hacha in Prague, seemed to be about to follow the example of the Slovaks and join in the war against Russia. What would Churchill make of all this, and indeed since America had entered the war after Pearl Harbor, President Roosevelt?

Heydrich had to be assassinated and the sooner the better. If his murder cost Czech blood that would be unfortunate, but it was a risk that had to be taken. Benes was cool and calculating. If Czechoslovakia were to be saved as an independent nation, after it had taken nearly three hundred years to attain that status once more in 1919, bitter sacrifices would have to be made and blood would have to flow.

Finally, on 28 December, 1941, Benes' problem was resolved. The bomber offensive against Germany started to pick up. It wouldn't be long before the new head of Bomber Command, Sir Arthur Harris, launched his first 1,000-bomber raid against the Reich. Bombers such as the Halifax, which had the range to get to Czechoslovakia and back, were at a premium. Even

[*] Goering, the pre-war author of Nazi Germany's Four Year Economic Plan, had already been very busy forcing large industrial complexes into his control. *Hermann-Goering Werke* were appearing all over Germany and the occupied territories.

so, a single squadron, the 138th, was assigned to the SOE for special duties. But it seemed that the Poles, with their very active 'Home Army' resistance movement, were to be given priority in the matter of aircraft. First the Poles and after them, possibly, the Czechs.

Then luck (or so it seemed at the time, but who knows today who arranged that 'luck'?) took a hand. On the morning 28 December, 1941, three days after Christmas, Flight Lieutenant Ron Hockey of 138 Squadron collected a brand new Halifax, the fuselage of which had been adapted to drop paratroops, from RAF Northolt. As the pilot recalled later: 'I went into the Met Office about lunchtime and thought there was a slim chance of doing a Czech op. that night. In view of the outstanding operations, I decided to try all three Halifaxes in the queue. In order to save time I alerted the Air Ministry Branch concerned and arranged to land at Tangmere to load. There was a reason for using Tangmere – the three groups of Czechs coming from near London.'

That afternoon a brief call alerted Moravec with the terse message: 'We're on.' Who telephoned him has never been explained, as several items that occurred that Christmas never have been.*

Moravec didn't waste a moment. He drove straight from his headquarters to Stanhope Terrace where Gabcik and Kubis were waiting for him. And there the trail stops as far as the Czech spymasters are concerned. All that we have from Colonel Moravec on what happened next are deliberate lies. The only truths seem to be in the wording of the brief conversation Moravec had with Sergeant Gabcik before he left. Why Moravec lied will never be known. Was he trying to present a more patriotic version of the para-agents' departure a quarter of a century after the events? Did he wish to rule out British involvement due to the political situation then pertaining in

---

* They probably never will be. The present-day Czech Government will not give the details, though the author knows that they had comprehensive files on the matter until comparatively recently. Neither will the British Foreign Office. As to whatever details the Germans tortured out of the Czechs after the assassination, they have disappeared for obvious reasons.

Czechoslovakia, though he personally had long fled once more to the West? Or had his mind gone? I think that very unlikely.

But, in the event, he gets the date of Gabcik's and Kubis's departure wrong by a good *four months*. He has the two of them meeting President Benes just before they left, though it's clear they didn't have time to do so in the rush to take advantage of the plane which had appeared, seemingly miraculously, when the Czechs least expected it. And finally there is no mention of the British pilot, Flight Lieutenant Hockey, whatsoever. In Moravec's account the assassins are flown by a Czech pilot, a Captain Andrle.

So what *do* we have from Colonel Moravec on his last moments with these young men? According to him, Gabcik said, 'Colonel, I'm embarrassed to tell you this, but I have a ten pound debt in our restaurant. Would it be possible for you to pay it for me?' This Moravec agreed to do. Thereupon Gabcik held out his hand and said, 'You can rely on us, Colonel. We shall fulfil our mission as ordered.' Good patriotic stuff, but sergeants offering their hands to full colonels! Well, perhaps the Czech wartime Army in exile was different from other armies I have known. And that was that. No mention of the RAF field from which they flew, the RAF bomber they used, nor the RAF pilot who flew them on the long, dangerous haul, and all, according to Moravec, *four months* later than the flight actually took place!

Already Hockey's engines in aircraft NF-V L9613 were idling on the tarmac at Tangmere, the airfield British Intelligence used for all its clandestine missions during the war. The parachutists waddled out to the tarmac. They had already been searched to ensure that they had nothing about their persons that might give them away if they were caught by the police, or, even worse, the Gestapo. There is no record that they were given one of the little throwaway flasks containing either whisky or cognac used to celebrate their safe arrival 'on the other side'. They were helped into the Halifax. Up in the cockpit Hockey gave the thumbs-up signal after testing his engines for one last time at full power.

The riggers didn't wait for a second invitation. It was freezing out there on the tarmac that December evening. They pulled away the chocks, the prop wash flattening their overalls against their bodies. Over in the tower a green light started to wink. It was the signal to roll. Hockey pulled back the throttles. The Halifax trembled with the sudden surge of power. In the rear the agents felt the fabric shake at their backs. In the tower the senior officers stood to attention. The CO saluted solemnly. It was the traditional send-off for brave young men, flying into the unknown, who might never return. The plane roared down between the lights of the flare path. The ANTHROPOID MISSION was on its way.

PART VI

'THE FINAL SOLUTION'

He who sups with the Devil must have a
long spoon.

1

There was no easing up for Hockey and his crew. The tension was palpable as they crossed the French border into Germany, getting a fix on the Saar River and heading up the Rhine for a while. But it wasn't only the enemy that worried Hockey, it was the plane's weight and speed. Including the crew, there were sixteen heavily laden men on board and there was as much fuel in the tanks as the crew chief dared load. After they'd made the DZ, there was the long journey back to Tangmere to contend with as well.

Near Darmstadt they ran into trouble. Two German night fighters appeared out of nowhere and started to trail the intruder. Fortunately the German *Nachtjäger* didn't seem to have airborne radar, which, though in its infancy, was still fairly effective, and they lost the Halifax.

Hockey began to turn south-east, following the River Elbe for a while, droning on steadily to Czechoslovakia. The weather worsened, but it gave them the cover they needed, though German air defences were thinner now because the RAF rarely penetrated this far into the Reich. All the same it made it more difficult for Hockey and his co-pilot to make out the landmarks they needed to direct them to the dropping zones assigned to the three para-teams.

The weather got steadily worse. As Hockey wrote in his flight log: 'Pinpointing became impossible owing to heavy snow which blotted out all roads, railways and small towns.' Even Staff Captain Sustr, who had volunteered to accompany the flight because he knew the area, couldn't identify any landmarks, although by now the bomber was flying at less than a thousand feet. Hockey realized that a decision would soon have to be made: either they dropped the agents blind or they returned home with them and tried again another day.

The decision was made. Originally it had been planned to drop the team somewhere near Pilsen. But by now the aircraft had penetrated well into Czechoslovakia, leaving the beer-brewing town to the west. In fact, unknown to the men on board waiting for the signal to jump, they were close to Prague. Captain Sustr, deciding that it would be very bad for Czech morale if he brought the three teams back, asked Hockey to take the bomber even lower. Although he disliked doing so, the pilot did as he was asked, coming down as low as five hundred feet in an attempt to get a 'visual' – a personal recognition of the DZ. But the weather was still against them. A moment later he lost his trailing aerial and knew, as he jerked the Halifax higher with an instinctive movement, that he ran a heavy risk of ramming the plane into the ground under these conditions.

But Captain Sustr asked him to try again; Hockey reluctantly agreed and started to come down once more. Suddenly the red light turned to green. Sustr had spotted their DZ!

In fact, he hadn't. He had instead made a snap decision, taking the responsibility upon himself. He decided that Gabcik and Kubis, the first to go, would be dropped at an approximate position. Sustr knew how so much depended upon their mission. He just had to take a chance, even if it involved endangering men's lives.

The two rose and slapped their bulky parachutes. Gabcik waddled to Sustr and, according to the latter's report, took the officer's hand, saying, 'Remember you will be hearing from us. We will do everything possible.'

Cold air rushed in. The two Czechs waited for the despatcher to give them the signal to go. The RAF NCO shouted something, but the words were snatched from his mouth by the wind. He slapped each one in turn on the shoulder. Then they were gone, pulled from the plane and towed beneath it by the

126

slipstream. The hatch was closed. The two Czech assassins were consigned irrevocably to the December darkness. Hockey recorded in his log, 'Dropped east of Pilsen at 02.24 on 29 December.' And that was that.

Gabcik floated down under his canopy, not knowing that he and Kubis were way off their DZ. In fact they were coming down near the village of Nehvidzy, some twenty kilometres from Prague. Kubis hit the ground in the correct position, rolled over and started to gather in his shroud lines as he had been taught. Gabcik was not so fortunate. He misjudged his height from the ground and hit it hard, hurting his left foot. Kubis ran over to his injured comrade, noting as he did so that this was not the planned DZ. Here there were no woods or hills in which they could hide until they made contact with the underground. Instead they were surrounded by bare, snow-covered fields, which afforded them no cover. But there was no time for recriminations. The main thing was to get out of sight before dawn. While the injured Gabcik started to scrape away painfully at the frozen snow in order to hide their parachutes, Kubis set off on a brief recce. It was his task to find a hiding place. He found a small hut; Gabcik hobbled to it and there they hid their equipment under a pile of empty potato sacks before eating a hasty meal of frozen-hard tinned corned beef and chocolate, which would give them the energy they'd need before they set off again. The hut would certainly not offer them the kind of cover they'd need.

Some time later they found an abandoned quarry with innumerable tunnels running from it. Here they made themselves at home, slipping deep into one of the tunnels, where they tried to keep warm and plan what to do next, especially as Gabcik obviously wouldn't be able to go very far with his injured foot.

Behind them they left a trail that in the winter dawn would be easy to follow: the scrape in which they had hidden their parachutes not very well; the trampled snow and the tracks leading to their present hiding place. It wouldn't take even a city-trained German policeman very long to find them. It seemed they had slipped up badly from the very start.

Inevitably they were discovered the following morning. Someone had followed their trail. He had been wakened by the drone of the Halifax, had later discovered the corned beef cans (very careless that) and then followed the footprints in the snow. He had uncovered something else, but the stranger kept that to himself for the time being.

He introduced himself as 'Baumann', said he was a game-keeper and told the two strangers that they were twenty kilometres outside Prague. Baumann was a common German name, but a lot of patriotic Czechs had German names. All the same, they were on their guard.

Then the gamekeeper – for he really was one – told them he had discovered the equipment they had hidden beneath the sacks. What was their 'little game'? They broke down and told him, upset, as they were, to find they were twenty kilometres from Prague. That meant they were cut off from their contact addresses in Pilsen.

But Baumann was not put out by the fact that they were agents and were asking for help, for in a way he too was connected with the Czech underground. He was a member of the *Sokol* organization, a patriotic group which sprang up wherever there were Czechs, even in America, and which Heydrich had declared illegal the previous year. Baumann now offered to contact the head of that organization, chemistry professor Vladislav Vanek, cover name 'Jindra', in Prague and ask for help.

Gabcik and Kubis knew that their present position was untenable. But they had been warned not to contact the Czech underground until their task was finished. There were too many traitors and German-paid infiltrators in the resistance. But they didn't really have any choice. In the countryside they would stick out like sore thumbs, especially as they were not native to the area and Gabcik needed time for his foot to heal. So they accepted Baumann's offer.

Over the New Year the Sokol operatives went to work. They brought the two para agents to Prague by a roundabout manner, where they met Professor Vanek.

Vanek, one of the few to survive the débâcle to come, allowed a week to pass before the meeting. In the meantime he had their papers examined. He was horrified with the result. Even the thickest Gestapo officer could have spotted that they were a fake. So they were changed and new ration books given to them.

When he did finally meet them Vanek was soon aware that Kubis didn't like the treatment he was receiving from the Sokol men one bit. But he couldn't help that. Gradually he pumped them about the people they had known in London until he was satisfied that they were genuine.

Then he tried to find out what they were up to. 'I asked Kubis what his mission was. He talked about some sort of special mission. Finally, after a lot of bluster, he said they were there to murder Heydrich.' That must have surprised Vanek, but, as he wrote afterwards, 'I'd suspected it all along especially after they mentioned their codeword ANTHROPOID. I have to admit that I was shocked. Because I knew what would happen if they were successful. Killing a pillar of the Nazi hierarchy would bring about horrific reprisals.'

But he could see that they hadn't thought about that. He tried to explain the situation, but his words had no effect. So he gave up. 'We had our orders from London and, as the underground organization on the spot, we had the duty of supporting them in the execution of the assassination the best we could.'

All the same, he didn't hurry the matter. He handed Kubis and Gabcik over to one of the best of the Sokol agents, a middle-aged, bespectacled teacher named Jan Zelenka, who went under the *nom de guerre* of 'Uncle Hajski'. For the time being, until Vanek knew more, 'Uncle' would look after them and prepare the ground for what was to come.

2

When he retired, Frantisek Safarik had been a cabinet-maker in Prague's Hradschin Castle for some forty years. From this humble position he would see the 'big shots' come and go. But nothing made such an impression on him as that day in the late winter of 1941/42 when he began to play a part, a very small one admittedly, in the history of his country.

It had started in the autumn. He had just taken a break from his work and was walking across the castle yard when he spotted a figure, bespectacled and grinning, who seemed familiar. The stranger appeared to think the same, for he stopped and came straight over to Safarik. Then the cabinet-maker recognized him. It was Mr Zelenka, his old schoolteacher. Zelenka, alias 'Uncle Hajski', held out his hand. 'Then he started questioning me like the old days back at school. He asked me what I thought of the new political situation. I told him I couldn't stand the Germans and that things were bad. The sort of stuff that one says on such occasions.'

The teacher listened carefully. Then 'he asked me to a drink and told me to call him by the "thou" form of address.'

Surprised a little by the offer – it wasn't usual for teachers to ask their former pupils to address them in the familiar manner – the cabinet-maker went along with 'Uncle Hajski', enjoyed his beer, answered a few more questions and that was about it. He supposed he'd never see Mr Zelenka again.

But he was wrong. A few days later he reappeared, as if by chance, just as Safarik was going off on his break. Later Safarik decided that there had been no chance involved; it had all been carefully planned. In the meantime the teacher had been making discreet enquiries about him.

This time Zelenka didn't beat about the bush. After a 'few questions, he asked me quite openly if I was prepared to do something for the resistance'. The cabinet-maker knew that if he answered in the affirmative he would be putting his head in the noose. He knew the Germans by now. They would stamp on a Czech like a beetle underfoot and he burned to pay them back for it. So he asked for a couple of days to think about it. When the teacher came back, he didn't hesitate. He said he'd help. Zelenka was obviously pleased and said he would be in touch again soon. And that was that.

By now Zelenka had turned Kubis and Gabcik over to a new-found 'aunt', namely Maria Moravec, nicknamed in resistance circles 'Auntie Marie'. Before he sent them to Auntie Marie's safe house, located in a large block of flats, no more than a hundred metres from his own place, Zelenka had given the two agents a thorough going-over. The papers he had already dealt with, but he was shocked by what he still found. Their civilian suits were English; their shirts and underwear still bore English laundry marks. They even carried English pound notes, which they showed around proudly. It was almost as if they didn't give a damn, as if they were quite certain that they were doomed. So what did it matter if their shirts and vests bore English laundry marks?

Zelenka thought it did. He got rid of all the English clothing and set about getting the necessary papers for them. He obtained employment books for them from friendly Czechs who worked in government offices; he brought in two doctors to certify that they couldn't work, which would stop them from being picked up and sent to work in the war industries by the Germans. He and Auntie Marie even introduced Kubis to a girl, Anna Malinova, whose husband had been killed by the Germans.

Life now settled down to a happy routine for the two would-be killers, or so it seemed. Auntie Marie often gave little parties to which they were invited. They didn't say much and the other guests suspected they were 'submarines' – people who had taken on a new identity because they had fallen foul of the Germans. All the same, they were remembered by those who met them at this time as cheerful, extrovert young men. When asked what they were up to they joked and said that they 'were counting ducks on the Vltava'. *

It was only with Auntie Marie's 21-year-old son Ata that they let their hair down when the three of them were alone. Ata, who worked as a courier for the Sokol, had a brother with the Czech Brigade in England and when he somehow learned that their two 'guests' had once belonged to that Brigade he started to ask questions with a look of almost hero-worship in his eyes. Fascinated by their weapons, which were hidden in the flat, and tales of Army life abroad, he soon found that they weren't just men trying to dodge conscription into the German war industry. They were here to carry out some specific task. But, outgoing as they were, Kubis and Gabcik never told Ata what that task was. Perhaps they were trying to protect him. If so they failed, for in the end Ata was to be subjected to the worst horrors of them all.

The weeks passed. January became February and the rigours of the winter slowly started to disappear. On the Eastern Front the Russians had stopped the Germans before Moscow and they had been forced to retreat. But really the fighting had bogged down thanks to 'General Winter', as the Russians called it. Still, the Germans had regained their confidence. They were preparing to go on the offensive again in the spring and there would inevitably be new tasks for Heydrich in the follow-up to that offensive. Things were afoot. Berlin was buzzing with rumours and he told Lina that he confidently expected to be called to the capital very soon.

It was about this time that Zelenka approached Safarik again; but not in person. Instead he relayed a message saying that he was sending him 'two young fellows' who'd like to have a chat with him. Naturally, the 'two young fellows' were Kubis and Gabcik. He liked them and in due course they told Safarik that they were parachutists sent specially from England.

* The river which runs through the capital.

The cabinet-maker did not record his reaction to the revelation, but he didn't hesitate when they started to ply him with questions about his boss, *Obergruppenführer* Reinhard Heydrich. In particular they wanted to know the details of his open-topped, high-speed Mercedes and the accompanying vehicle of the SS bodyguard which often, though not always, followed it. In the end, 'they asked me to show them the Mercedes and the other car.' He did and 'told them everything else they wanted to know.'

After that they started to appear in the courtyard at frequent intervals. 'Sometimes they even came with their girlfriends . . . and then, one day, they told me that they were going to kill Heydrich.'

By now the two assassins-to-be were deep into their preparations for the murder and were in radio contact with Moravec in London once more. Although the information that they were there to kill Heydrich seemed to Sarafik 'to stink like the grave-yard', and he told them so, they continued with their plans.

Heydrich moved around a lot. Often his movements seemed to be spontaneous, made, it appeared, on the spur of the moment. But Kubis and Gabcik needed to know his specific schedule if they were ever going to kill him. So they broadened their search.

They started to haunt the road from the Heydrich home at Panenske Brezany. They cultivated another agent, unknown to Sarafik, a watchmaker named Josef Novotny, who repaired watches for the German garrison and he told them all he knew of the Germans' routine as far as it affected Heydrich.

They even penetrated Heydrich's home, which was not too difficult. Frau Heydrich had acquired the haughty manner of a *grande dame*. She simply didn't see her servants. As long as they took care of the seventy rooms that were her lot, ensured that she could go off hunting with the local German gentry (she had even taken the difficult German *Jagdschein**) and looked after her children she was well satisfied and let them go about their business.

* Hunting Licence, a very complicated procedure, complete with difficult examination, even today.

Thus it was not difficult for the underground to penetrate the *Heydrich-Residenz*, find out what they wanted to know, even rifle through the *Obergruppenführer*'s wastepaper baskets. Bit by bit Kubis and Gabcik put Heydrich's daily schedule together under the very noses of the SS guard permanently assigned to him.

It didn't take the two would-be killers long to realize that Heydrich could be assassinated neither at Panenske Brezany nor at his HQ at the castle. At both they would be too vulnerable and the SS would be in a position to take up the chase at once.

As Zelenka said after the war, 'The country round Panenske Breznay offered not the least possibility of hiding or getting away. For those who carried it out, an attempt in this place would certainly have meant suicide.' And by now neither Kubis nor Gabcik wanted to die. They were young men, back in their homeland, admired by those who knew what they had come to do. And both had steady girlfriends, whom they intended to marry after the war, one of whom was already pregnant! After years on the run they had found a kind of peace. They'd kill the tyrant all right, but they wanted to survive that killing.

3

At his trial in Jerusalem long after, the bespectacled German told his captors, 'I regarded the Jews with respect . . . to whom a mutually acceptable, a mutually fair solution had to be found.' It is not recorded what Adolf Eichmann's Jewish listeners made of that statement. Was it the height of hypocrisy or had he really meant it? Had he genuinely attempted to find a solution in the form of a new homeland where they wouldn't suffer the fate that the Nazis had seemingly reserved for them?

Whatever the truth, by the summer of 1941 he knew that there was no chance of resettling the Jews, neither in Madagascar nor anywhere in the East, now under German control. They would be resettled in the new ghettoes the SS had created, worked for the benefit of Himmler's economic empire until they could work no longer and then disposed of. In August of that year he was summoned by Heydrich and told 'The Führer has ordered the extermination of the Jews'.

According to his testimony at his 1961 trial, 'At first I was unable to grasp the significance of what he said because he was so careful in choosing his words, and then I understood and didn't say anything, because there was nothing to say anymore. I had never thought of such a thing, such a solution through violence. I now lost everything, all joy in my work, all initiative, all interest.'

But by that August Eichmann knew that the cause of Zionism which he apparently thought he was pursuing had been a cover for genocide for those Jews unable to provide either labour or capital for the SS.

Despite his lack of enthusiasm, it didn't seem to take Eichmann long to adapt to the new situation. He was sent to Lublin to get acquainted with the SS's use of gas to suffocate the Jews to death. 'I became physically weak,' he said to his judges. Still *Befehl ist Befehl* (orders are orders). He continued with his course of instruction in the mechanics of death. Off he went to Chelmno to witness the latest innovation: mobile gas vans. Passing through Lvov, he claimed that he had told a local SS commander, 'What is being done around here is horrible. Young people are being turned into sadists. How can one do that? That is impossible. Our people will go mad.'

But the Germans didn't go mad and Eichmann had finished his apprenticeship in death. *Der Experte* was ready to get down to some serious mass murder. All he needed was the green light, which he was to receive from Heydrich on 20 January, 1942, at a discreet house in Berlin. It had once been the home of the German section of Interpol. Now the *Villa am Grossen Wannsee* No 56–58 was to be the setting of the conference which would lead to the greatest mass murder in history.

Heydrich opened by reeling off the figures of Jews put to death so far, before going on to the problem which had occupied himself and Eichmann for so long – Jewish emigration. By the end of October, 1941, he told his audience, 537,000 Jews had 'emigrated'. Unfortunately the war had put an end to that. In its place, 'with the Führer's agreement, a possible solution of the Jewish problem is the large-scale dispatch of Jews to the new eastern territories.' Most of those present, including the frock-coated gentlemen from von Ribbentrop's Foreign Ministry, did not need a crystal ball to know what Heydrich meant. 'Dispatch' was simply a euphemism for the mass murder of the Jews soon to come in the East.

Eichmann, as a half-colonel in the SS, was probably the lowest ranking person at that conference, the only one dealing with mass murder that has been recorded in detail; three protocols of the Wannsee Conference survive. So it must have flattered him when Heydrich invited him to stay behind with Müller for an informal chat about what should be done next.

136

Obviously his two bosses needed his expert advice. They didn't want to bother themselves with the trivia of genocide. They told him that he was to ensure that the Jewish Elders used their own police to select those who were to be sent to the extermination camps, where the new apparatus of death (including Zyklon B gas, invented and produced by *IG Farbenwerke*, which belonged to the 'Friends of *Reichsführer SS* Himmler') would speedily deal with them. The Final Solution could begin.

But what of Heydrich? What was his reaction to this final infamy? It has been shown since that he was careful to ensure that words such as 'killing' 'extermination', 'liquidation' and the like were eradicated from the final protocols. Was he covering his tracks? Was he ashamed of what he was ordering his subordinates to do? Hardly likely. Shame was not part of his make-up.

Although he detested and despised the Jews for personal reasons known only to himself, and naturally for professional reasons as well, he knew the power of what he would have called 'International Jewry'. It is my guess that he didn't want to appear before so many potential witnesses as the originator of the programme of mass extermination. In essence, he seems to have made it appear that the people really responsible for the plan were the Führer and Field Marshal Goering, who saw the Jewish problem as part of his pre-war 'Four Year Plan'. Again it was a question of economics and not mere anti-semitism.

Be that as it may, it was almost the last time that Heydrich would step into the pages of the history books. For already his fate was sealed. His days were numbered and the world would always associate him with the Wannsee Conference and the fact that he appeared to have been the author of the Final Solution. According to Lina this was unfair. She remembers her husband at that time adopting a totally different point of view. After the conference the two of them discussed it in what she described as a 'very objective manner'. He said that he was preparing for the emigration of all Jews to Central Russia. She asked him, 'You're saying that all Jews are going to be deported to Siberia?' 'Yes, I'm saying that exactly. But Siberia isn't the land of terror you think. It's only because the Russians

137

used it for their punishment camps that it has gained its terrible reputation. Remember what Major von Pomme told us about Siberia?' He was referring to an acquaintance who had been a Russian POW in Siberia during the First World War. 'He always told his son that Siberia was a place he'd always like to return to as a free man. It is a wonderful country.'

Heydrich rambled on about the mineral wealth, the coal and ore resources of Siberia until Lina interrupted him. 'But can the Jews cope with the wilderness?'

'Yes. They are an intelligent people. I shall introduce them to Siberia carefully.' He pointed out on a map the area he had assigned to the Jews which prompted Lina to remark, 'But those areas haven't even been conquered by the *Wehrmacht* yet.'

He nodded and that was that. But for the rest of her life Lina stuck firmly to the belief that her husband, acting on orders from 'higher authority', ie the Führer and Goering, had organized a not too important conference on the resettlement of Jews somewhere in Siberia. He did not want to exterminate them, as the world supposed. On the contrary, he wanted to give them a fresh start in that land of milk and honey yet to be conquered.

VII

DEATH OF A TYRANT

'I don't say he's a great man . . . he's not
the finest character that ever lived. But
he's a human being and a terrible thing is
happening to him. So attention must be
paid. He's not to be allowed to fall into his
grave like an old dog. Attention, attention
must be finally paid to such a person.'

Arthur Miller.

1

'Now we're ready,' they had told Zelenka back in March, 1942. Although he didn't like to show his emotions, the head of the Sokol Organization in Prague was appalled. His organization was at grave risk as it was. The Gestapo had captured one of his radio operators and then taken several other members prisoner. Sooner or later they would talk. Now the para-agents wanted to go ahead with the assassination and he knew quite well that an attempt on Heydrich's life, even if it were unsuccessful, would create hell on earth for the Czechs. He had begged for time to check with London. London's answer was laconic: 'Go ahead'.

Later Zelenka said, 'It was obvious that London wanted to prove that the Czechoslovak people had nothing to do with Hacha's puppet government in Prague. We had to be seen as resisting. At the same time London wanted the reprisals that would follow an assassination of that nature to challenge and activate the resistance. Two months later, in May, 1942, Jan Kubis and Gabcik informed me that they had found a spot for the assassination and explained their plan.' And he had to admit that it was a good plan. They had toyed with such crazy ideas as sneaking into Heydrich's bedroom and slitting his throat or garrotting him while he slept, with Lina presumably sleeping tamely at his side. This plan was different, however.

Meanwhile, Sokol, worried about the consequences of the assassination, contacted London again. This time 'the

141

President talked to Colonel Moravec, who left the meeting with the direct order of the President, the highest commander of the army, immediately to instruct the parachutists to abandon their mission.'

Colonel Moravec's depiction of this last, crucial phase of the ANTHROPOID operation is different. According to him he received Sokol's plea to abandon the op and 'I took it to President Benes and the Chief of British Intelligence, Stewart Menzies*. President Benes ordered me not to answer. The Chief of the SIS did not say anything, but I have learned since the war that the British . . . insisted on the execution of the order.'

Again Moravec fudged the issue, *afterwards*. After the assassination, he, like the other leading Czechs in exile, wanted to pass the buck. So the now dead Menzies was named as the man who gave the final go-ahead for the assassination. We might well ask why Menzies would have given his sanction to an operation that wouldn't particularly benefit Britain. More important, however, is the fact that we know that the operation never came before the JIC; yet the first political assassination attempted by any side during the war would surely have been important enough for that Committee to review it and give its approval or otherwise?

In other words, it looks as if Moravec was again distorting the facts and, even thirty years after the event, attempting to shift the blame to anyone but himself and Benes. But the real proof of the pudding is this: *if President Benes didn't approve of the Heydrich assassination, why didn't he cancel it*? But he didn't! Come what may, the killing of *Obergruppenführer* Reinhard Heydrich was to go ahead.

The plan worked out by Kubis and Gabcik was relatively simple. The two assassins had found out that Heydrich travelled between Panenske Brezany every day, leaving shortly after nine in the morning and heading for his office at the Hradcany Castle in Prague in an open Mercedes, travelling

* Later Sir Stewart Menzies, who allegedly shot himself some years after the war as a result, some maintain, of Philby's defection to the Russians and the activities of other traitors within his organization.

well above the official speed limit. The assassination would take place in the suburb of Holesovice. There was a crossroads, with a sharp bend on a hill, which led down to the Traja Bridge. It was at this spot that Klein, Heydrich's driver, would have to slow down and change gear in order to take the bend before taking the hill. The Mercedes, with its passenger either in the back or in the front seat next to the driver-cum-bodyguard (Heydrich was apt to use either seat as the fancy took him) would be an ideal target here.

And here Heydrich would be at his most vulnerable. He would be cut off from both the SS platoon at his country home and the SS battalion stationed on guard-and-watch duties at Hradcany Castle. Nor were there any Czech police posts or German Army barracks in the neighbourhood, and after the assassination the killers would be off on their bicycles and on their way to their safe houses before the Germans knew what had happened.

To anyone surveying the scene of the assassination to come it would all look perfectly normal, Gabcik reasoned. The various tram stops at the corner would allow them to loiter there without arousing suspicion as if they were ordinary civilians waiting for a tram. Up ahead of the two killers themselves a third member of the team from London, Vaclik would signal the arrival of the Mercedes by flashing a pocket mirror. Gabcik would then assemble his British Sten machine pistol and as soon as Heydrich came within range he would open fire. Once Heydrich went down and the car came to a halt, Kubis, who carried two Mills grenades, would dash forward, grab the dead man's briefcase as proof that they had really killed him, whereupon they would make a run for it.

Crude and desperate the plan might be, but it had the beauty of simplicity and the advantage that it involved only three people.

Still the plotters of the Sokol movement hesitated. But events were running away with them. There was little time left for discussion. Besides they were under orders from London to get on with the job. Weren't they soldiers in a way? Could they disobey those orders as civilians in uniform? When the war was won and the Czechs were in power once again, as the Sokol men fervently hoped they would be, wouldn't they be laying themselves open to charges of insubordination, disobedience, even refusal to carry out an order – all serious offences under the military code of conduct? Dare they risk that?

They decided they couldn't. Whatever their private thoughts were that last crucial week of May, they kept them to themselves and decided to give their support to the Gabcik plan of assassination.

Meanwhile things were moving fast for Heydrich too. There was talk that he was to take charge in Belgium and Occupied France and stamp out resistance there; also that 'at the same time he is to act as supervisor of the Vichy government' (the French government of Unoccupied France). In the meantime he was to proceed to Berlin anyway. There he was to inspect a parade of *Waffen-SS Fahnenjunker* (officer cadets) before reporting personally to the Führer.

All this the plotters learned from the clock-maker Josef Novotny who had access to Heydrich's office. He had discovered that Heydrich was scheduled to leave for Berlin within the next few days and it was rumoured among his staff that he might not return. If Hitler decided the transfer was urgent enough, he would move to the West without further ado, his wife and family following in due course. The time for action had come.

Now, on the evening of 26 May, Heydrich celebrated one final triumph. It was a homage to his father, Bruno Suess-Heydrich, the supposed half-Jew who had never been accepted by middle-class German society. Heydrich had arranged a concert of his father's half-forgotten chamber music for the inaugural programme of the Prague Musical Festival. The music would be played by a quartet of his former pupils of the Halle Conservatory. Heydrich had even written the programme notes himself. What an honour! Bruno Heydrich's music to be played where once Mozart and Beethoven had performed! What a feeling it must have been for his son as he strode, his wife on his arm, into the concert hall. It must have been one of the most sublime moments of his life.

144

2

May 27, 1942, dawned cool and a little hazy. After the previous night, when a great deal of champagne had been drunk Heydrich was a little slow in his movements and it was not until just before ten o'clock that he was ready to leave for Prague, before going to the airfield for the flight to Berlin. He said goodbye to Lina and the children, but before he left he said to Lina, 'Frank's days are numbered.' He was referring to Karl Frank*, who, Heydrich felt, was enriching himself in Prague. Klein, standing next to the Mercedes, clicked to attention and Heydrich got in. Then they set off. They sped through the hamlet of Predboj. Before them was a road sign which read *'Praha 16 km'*. At this rate they should be in the capital in ten minutes. That would please the *Gruppenführer*.

In the suburb of Holesovice, where the Dresden-Prague road took the hairpin bend down to the Traja Bridge, the assassins were also worried about the time. They had taken up their posts before nine, the time at which Heydrich usually set off. He should have been here before now. Was he coming or not?

Kubis looked across at Gabcik. He was standing there, Sten hidden beneath his coat. His comrade looked perfectly normal. But he knew Gabcik would be as nervous as he was. He looked up the road to where Vaclik was hidden, but nothing was happening.

Then suddenly Vaclik's mirror flashed. It was 10.32.

---

* Karl Hermann Frank, not to be confused with Gauleiter Hans Frank, Governor-General of the Central Polish territory not annexed by Russia or Germany.

145

Heydrich was on his way! There was a noise as Klein changed down at speed. Gabcik slid the automatic from beneath his coat. Kubis dropped his briefcase, part of his camouflage as a worker waiting for a tram. He grabbed a grenade and clutched it in a wet hand. A low, green open car swept into view. There was no mistaking the man with the gleaming cap and the insignia of the SS above its peak. Heydrich was sitting next to the driver.

Gabcik dropped his raincoat and brought up the cheap gun. He pressed the trigger. At this range he couldn't miss. But nothing happened. He pressed again. Still nothing. The gun had jammed!

Gabcik just stood gaping, almost within touching distance of the two men in the car. Now they'd spotted him and now Heydrich made his fatal mistake. He grabbed for his Walther automatic and sprang to his feet. He yelled to Klein, '*Anhalten! Los!*'

Klein hit the brakes. Neither he nor Heydrich had spotted Kubis; they thought they were dealing with just one man. The car screeched to a halt just in front of Kubis. He reacted correctly, and at once. He stepped out of the shadows, his mind working as if on automatic pilot. Two seconds delay, don't throw so hard in case the bomb bounces off, just lob it into the front. He ran three strides towards the car and lobbed his grenade. But he misjudged it. The grenade hit the rear wheel and exploded. Shrapnel pinged everywhere. Kubis was hit in the face. Blood streamed down his face, half-blinding him. All around civilians screamed. The shrapnel had shattered the windows of a nearby tram which clanged to a halt. In a flash all was chaos.

Kubis lost his head. As smoke started to pour from the wrecked Mercedes, he ran towards his bike and swung himself into the saddle, the blood blinding him still. The panic-stricken crowd rushing from the tram got in his way. He raised his Colt.45 and fired into the air.

Behind him Klein, his automatic drawn, took up the chase. He fired, regardless of the crowd. A click and his magazine fell out. In his confusion he had pressed the magazine release catch! Kubis didn't wait for him to recover. He started to pedal from the scene of the crime and in moments was going full tilt, heading downhill.

Meanwhile Heydrich, seemingly unaware that he had been hit, was after Gabcik, who had slung away his useless Sten and was trying to reach his bike. But Heydrich was still after him, swaying crazily like a new-born foal, trying to remain upright on weak legs. Gabcik took cover behind a telegraph pole and started to fire at Heydrich. A regular little battle ensued. Desperately, the Czech assassin sought a way out. It would only be a matter of moments before the cops arrived and that would be that.

Suddenly Heydrich keeled over, clutching his side. He managed to raise himself as Klein came panting up. 'Get that bastard,' he gasped. So Klein ran on after Gabcik. Behind him Heydrich staggered a few steps, then collapsed over the bonnet of the Mercedes, blood spurting from his side. Nobody helped him. The crowd just gaped at him in shock. He was a German. What had it got to do with them?

Gabcik had a chance now. He turned into a side street, the clatter of heavy boots behind him indicating that Klein was still after him. He ran into a butcher's shop. A fellow Czech would aid him, he reasoned, but he couldn't have been more mistaken. The butcher, Bauer, was a Nazi sympathizer. He even had a brother who worked for the Gestapo. He ignored Gabcik's plea for help and rushed into the street shouting, 'He's in here!'

Klein rushed into the shop and collided with Gabcik, trying to get out. Gabcik fired his Colt and Klein fell to the floor, shot in both legs.

Gabcik ran out of the shop, but Klein hadn't given up. As Gabcik tried to force his way through the crowd, he handed his pistol to Bauer and told him to take up the chase. But the butcher hesitated. The crowd were all Czechs. They were apathetic now, but what would they be like on the morrow? He let the pistol droop in his hand. Moments later Gabcik disappeared from sight.

3

Hitler was informed two hours later. The news of the assassination reached him at his headquarters on the Eastern Front just after midday and he flew into a rage. 'Stupidity and criminal carelessness,' he yelled at the messenger. His anger was directed at Heydrich and those responsible for his safety. Twenty minutes later, at half past twelve, he called Frank in Prague to find out whether Heydrich was still alive.

He was, and apparently he owed his life to a Czech! A young woman at the scene had recognized him. She yelled for help and an off-duty policeman had stopped a passing baker's van. The driver had been reluctant to get involved, but the cop persuaded him and off they went, with Heydrich squeezed into the back, bleeding heavily. At eleven they reached the Bulkova Hospital. Here a young Czech doctor, Dr Vladimir Snajdr got Heydrich into the operating theatre, but Heydrich had regained his usual icy composure and refused a painkilling shot. He ordered the Czech to attend his wounds as he was. Then, according to Frank, a German medic, a Dr Dick, had taken over. He didn't think the wound was too grave. Still, he recommended an operation. This was now being carried out by a Nazi doctor, a Professor Hohlbaum.

Hitler ordered reprisals at once. A million mark reward was ordered for the capture of the assassins. Anyone helping them escape was to be shot out of hand. Finally, 10,000 Czechs were to be arrested at once as hostages and all Czech political prisoners already under arrest were to be shot immediately. The

Czechs, had to be shown who was master in Prague.

When Himmler reported to Hitler a little later his temper was even worse. If the Czechs didn't like Heydrich he'd send them someone they really could hate. He infected Himmler with his mood. After the latter had dispatched his own personal surgeon to look after 'our good Reinhard', he also called Frank and told him to arrest some of the Czech intelligentsia and 'shoot this very night one hundred of the most important'.

That night the Germans imposed a nine o'clock curfew on Prague. Battalions of SS, Gestapo, *Wehrmacht* infantry – some 21,000 men in all – moved in to check 36,000 houses. They were in full battle order and ready to open fire at a moment's notice. The great search netted over five hundred 'suspects'. None of them was very important, save a Jan Zika, a member of the Czech Communist Party's Central Committee (that pleased Benes, for he feared the communists as much as he did the Germans). But there was absolutely no trace of the assassins.

Meanwhile Heydrich fought for his life. At first the prognosis had been good. The shrapnel from Kubis' bomb seemed to have missed any major internal organs. Spine and kidneys had not apparently been damaged; the wounds were, so it seemed in the preliminary examination, superficial. But the subsequent X-rays changed all that. They revealed that he *had* suffered internal injuries. He had a broken rib, a ruptured diaphragm and splinters had been forced into his spleen. The latter were the most serious. In an age of no real antibiotics or penicillin, the onset of gas gangrene or other infections of the wound could not be stopped once they had started. Then it was a case of cutting away flesh and yet more flesh in a race to beat the infection before it took over the whole body. That was why Professor Hohlbaum was now preparing to operate. He'd clean out the splinters before they had time to set about destroying his illustrious patient.

In the meantime Inspector Pannwitz of the Gestapo had been to visit his chief before he was taken into the operating theatre and was appalled by what he found. The *Obergruppenführer* was alone save for two nurses applying icepacks to his forehead in order to keep his temperature down. Immediately he had ordered a squad of SS to surround the building; then he

149

drove to the scene of the crime and secured it. Immediately the woman's bicycle (Auntie Marie's), two briefcases, a fused bomb of British manufacture, the Sten, a coat and a handful of cartridges (again British) were brought to him for examination. He didn't need to waste much time on them. He surmised immediately that the plotters had been armed and probably sent by the British: 'Because the sub-machine gun was also British, there was no doubt as to where the assassination had been organized.'

Now, with the Bulkova Hospital surrounded by armed SS men and no Czech allowed within fifty metres of Heydrich and the operating theatre, Doctors Dick and Hohlbaum set about repairing the damage. They were 'optimistic', as they reported to Himmler who now began calling the hospital every hour to enquire about 'dear Reinhard'. But there was one complication. Heydrich seemed to be developing blood poisoning. Still, they thought they could cure it. Thereafter it should be plain sailing. They were to be proved wrong, but Heydrich, although in agony, would fight off death for seven days.

In the world outside the *Obergruppenführer*'s sterile sick room, Germany was notching up great victories. In Russia the Germans were driving the Russians back once more, the latter suffering heavy losses. In North Africa Rommel was at the top of his form. Soon he would capture Tobruk after only a few days of siege, sending Churchill into a fit of despair, and then set out to conquer Cairo.

But, despite these tremendous events, all the real talk in both the German and enemy camps, was about Heydrich. Between 1936 and 1942 the London *Times* had mentioned him a mere nine times. Now it dealt with him every day. But it was clear that *The Times*, which was very close to the British government, knew as little about the attempted murder as the German authorities. Was this another indication that the British government had had nothing to do with the affair, as Bentinck's letter suggests? Indeed *The Times* pointed out that 'it won't be the first time. . . . Is Heydrich the first of another vendetta in the Nazi camp?' The reference was to the shooting of the SA leaders by Hitler during the 'Roehm' Putsch of 1934.

The *Manchester Guardian*, then still published in

Manchester, with its sizeable Jewish community, pointed out that it was 'bad news', implying further reprisals for Czechs and Jews. The *Guardian* was right. The reprisals had already begun. But there was much worse to come. England still did not comprehend the full brutality of Germany's brown-clad masters. After three years of war Britain's politicians had not realized that they were not dealing with people like themselves. This was not the customary gentleman's business of questions in the House, parliamentary papers, motions of confidence and so on. They were dealing with ruthless killers who laughed at the British and their quaint ideas.

The Nazis wanted the culprits to be punished; the whole Czech nation should atone for this heinous crime committed against one of their own. And it seems that Czech officialdom in London were little better. If the Czech people back in the homeland were not prepared to fight the occupier, then they would have to suffer in the cause of Czech freedom. It was a *marcher ou crever* situation – *march or croak*.

4

The last sighting of Gabcik was made by the Family Fafeky. On the 27th, after his flight from the shop, he had taken a tram to their home in the Prague suburb of Zizkov, where he had a stiff drink and then proceeded to lighten his hair with a dye solution. Kubis had fled to Auntie Marie's flat, but he could only stay there for a short time. Then he'd have to find another safe house. The only hope for him, and Gabcik, wherever he was, was to get out of Prague as soon as possible and then out of the country.

During the next thirty-six hours the two were passed from safe house to safe house. Sokol managed to retrieve the blood-stained bicycle from the scene of the crime, but the girl who was sent to fetch it was spotted, traced and finally arrested.

The Professor knew that something had to be done quickly. The Germans were staging snap raids all over Prague and the culprits would be caught sooner or later. They had to be hidden somewhere central so that they could be reached swiftly and spirited out of Prague as soon as he found a way of doing so.

In the end he resorted to a kind of medieval sanctuary. He approached Dr Vladimir Petrek of the Czech Orthodox Church who agreed to hide the paras in the centrally located St Cyril and Methodius Church where they could be hidden in the crypt. One by one the paras were smuggled in by Petrek, a lay preacher, and the other churchmen who swore on the altar never to betray their fellow Czechs. They were brought in ones and twos, Gabcik being brought in last.

Immediately they set about making the underground chambers habitable. They laid in stores of food, water and vodka. They asked for more ammunition for the weapons which they had smuggled in with them. It was almost as if they were unconsciously preparing for the siege which would come soon enough. But they didn't know that then. All around them the Germans were arresting people just for their looks or because they had forgotten to bring their pass with them. Men and women were being shot all the time and the German-controlled papers printed long lists of those who had been killed.

But in their underground asylum the paras knew nothing of this. They smoked and slept a lot, the classic signs of men mentally and nervously exhausted. After the first excitement of the reunion, they had talked of what had happened to them since the drop. But that soon wore off and thereafter they chatted lazily like men who had all the time in the world, though all their thoughts were centred on how long it would take Sokol to get them out.

Time and again the priests reassured them, they would just have to be patient. Everything was being taken care of. Due to intense German activity, all radio contact with London had been lost save one. Over this President Benes had sent his congratulations: 'I thank you sincerely. I can see that you and your friends are absolutely determined. It is proof to me that the whole nation is solidly together. I can assure you it will bring success. The events over there have a great effect here and attract attention for the resistance of the Czech people.' And that was the last the young men heard from their President.

But Benes, was using the attempted assassination for all it was worth. It pleased him immensely that it was headline news in the British and American papers. In Hollywood they were even talking of making a movie of the attack. *But there was

---

* On the 28th Fritz Lang, the master of the *cinema noir*, and the exiled German writer Berthold Brecht were walking along a beach in California when the latter suggested a movie of the event. Subsequently the two fell out, but the movie was made, *Hangmen Also Die*, with, ironically, a German-Jewish actor playing Heydrich.

one fly in the ointment for the Czechs. One of the original para-agents could not be found. He was Sergeant Karel Curda and he had broken all the rules laid down by his SOE trainers right from the start. Instead of seeking shelter from strangers, as they had recommended, he had headed straight for his parents' remote farm in Southern Bohemia, the centre of pre-war influence in Czechoslovakia.*

Now that the balloon had gone up Curda had panicked. Some time after 27 May he had fled once more to Southern Bohemia and was now hiding in his mother's barn. His seven comrades hiding in the crypt didn't know this yet, but the Professor did and he was worried. How would Curda behave now he didn't have the support of the underground and with only his mother to rely on for advice? A friend of Gabcik and Kubis, he knew all about the Heydrich operation, including the names and addresses of their underground friends and helpers. Would he crack?

In Berlin, Dr Goebbels, the Minister of Propaganda and Public Enlightenment, was pulling out all the stops. His radio stations and the press were screaming tirades of rage at the British for this 'dastardly murder attempt'. But the Germans could do little against the 'perifidious English', so Goebbels turned the hate on to the 'treacherous Czechs'. Daily the media demanded ever more drastic penalties. If they did not surrender the would-be killers soon they must face the consequences of their actions. In Prague the police trucks never appeared to cease rolling as they headed back and forth to the jails bearing the victims of the firing squads and the dreaded guillotines.

Heydrich naturally knew nothing of this. He was still fighting for his life, though the German doctors at the Bulova Hospital felt he was now out of danger. They had taken him off the 'very critically ill' list, in the hope that his youth and his physical condition would carry him through. By now, as May gave way

* There had been a disruptive and sizeable minority in the east of the country which, after Hitler came to power, had demanded to return to Germany: *Heim ins Reich*. That part of Czechoslovakia was riddled with German settlements.

to June, he was beginning to receive a handful of visitors. Himmler came, as did the detested Frank. Schellenberg, who might well have thought that Heydrich's illness would provide him with a means of advancement, did not visit his old chief. The powers-that-be were confident that one day Heydrich would be able to resume his duties.

Lina, true to her North German upbringing where any display of emotion is looked down upon, did not agree with the doctors' optimistic prognosis. She felt that there was something seriously wrong with her husband. As she wrote afterwards, 'Suddenly I didn't know the man I had been married to for the last eleven years. He seemed to have accepted his condition with a kind of easiness that might well have been the result of the drugs they had given him. Today I am inclined to believe that he had lost the will to live.' She noted that, 'He wasn't scared, but he hadn't the energy to live on. I couldn't understand this attitude from a man who had once been a bundle of energy and strength of purpose.'

Lina then came up with an analysis of her dying husband's personality which has never occurred to his dozen or so postwar biographers. As she put it some thirty years after the event, when she had been reduced to the role of the owner of a humble beachside café on her native island of Fehmarn, 'I always thought he had lived with the idea that he wouldn't grow old, but would have to die young. . . . I know it is somewhat trite, but I believe that he wished to sacrifice himself. Why else did he, in his position, undertake the many dangerous air force missions when he didn't need to? They were the beginning of this death wish.'

Lina might well have been right. In postwar Germany there would be no place for killers like Heydrich. The bankers, the industrialists, the businessmen, who would run the country, as they were, in part, already doing, would see to that. Extremists like Heydrich weren't good for business! Perhaps he did realize that his time had come. It was better to die now when he was at the height of his power and still respected.

On 2 June, 1942, with the killers still at liberty, Himmler himself came to visit his dying subordinate. Once, it was said, the *Reichsführer SS* had been afraid of Heydrich. Not now.

Indeed, he had only two more days to live.

According to Lina, Himmler said that Reinhard had 'received him well; he had even seemed a little happy'. But that is about all we know of that last conversation between the two men who had brought fear and death to half of Europe. The pair of them who, more even than Hitler, would blacken Germany's reputation for decades, left no record of those last words. But Lina did record that Himmler said one more thing about that final meeting. He said that Heydrich had 'declaimed to him in a firm voice' a verse from one of his dead father's operas, *The Barrel Organ*. It went: 'The world is just a barrel organ, which the Lord God turns himself. All of us have to dance to the tune engraved on the drum.'

Thirty-six hours later Heydrich closed his eyes for the last time.

VIII

FINALE

Your visitation shall receive such thanks
As fits a king's remembrance.

Shakespeare.

1

Karel Curda cracked first. The Germans had set an ultimatum on the day that Heydrich died. If the Czechs didn't deliver the killers to the Reich authorities by 16 June the Czech nation would suffer a terrible fate. On the very day that that proclamation was issued the Gestapo and the *Wehrmacht* made their first reconnaissance of the small mining village of Lidice. An example was going to be set and Lidice would go down in history, not for anything its villagers had done during their lifetime but by the manner of their death.

On 9 June at 19.45 the local Gestapo received a telephoned order from Karl Frank in Berlin to deal with the 'terrorist nest' of Lidice. All the male inhabitants were to be shot; all children who could be 'aryanized' on account of their Germanic appearance were to be sent to the Reich to be adopted by childless German couples; the village itself was to be burned to the ground. Those who were left over were to be dispatched to Ravensbruck Concentration Camp immediately.*

The constant shootings, and now the destruction of Lidice, seem to have been too much for Curda, hiding out in his

---

* Lidice's fate shocked the western world. Gerald Kersch, a popular writer of the time, wrote a novel about the place. A Welsh mining village changed its name to Lidice for a while and, even today, English mining villages keep in touch and help the post-war reconstructed Lidice.

mother's barn. He lost his nerve and accepted an offer, also put out by Frank, with the prompting of *Oberkommissar* Pannwitz. Anyone helping to identify the killers would get a reward of a million marks *and* would come to no harm.

Among the 2,000 letters and statements received from Czechs in the first three days after the new offer there was an anonymous letter mailed to the Czech police at the small town of Bensov. It stated: 'Cease searching for the assassins of Heydrich; cease arresting and executing innocent people. I can't stand it any more. The perpetrators of the assassination are a certain Gabcik from Slovakia and Jan Kubis, whose brother is an innkeeper.'

The letter was from Curda. Why he sent it no one really knows. In the three years left before the postwar Czech government had him hanged he seemed almost mad. At his trial and subsequent execution he certainly was. But that was later.

Anyway Curda was now out to save himself. That letter was the first stage. When it produced no immediate result he took what was left of his courage in both hands, travelled to the capital and walked into the Prague HQ of the Gestapo at the Petek Palais. He caught the cops by surprise and for a while they believed his initial story, that he had information about one of the briefcases left behind by the fleeing assassins. Not for long, however. The Germans soon realized that this was a 'big fish' which had turned up so unexpectedly in their net. Within half an hour they had wheeled him in to face no less a person than *Oberkommissar* Heinz Pannwitz.

Pannwitz could have gone through the usual treatment with a suspect, one that dated back to the Kaiser's days. It was called *die erste Abreibung* and entailed knocking the prisoner about a bit before he was interrogated. Nothing serious, not even vindictive, just a couple of cops cuffing and punching the prisoner in a half-hearted manner in order to soften him up for the real interrogation to come. Pannwitz may have used threats as well, advising the suspect that he might well have to apply to the *Reichsführer SS** to use *'scharfer Arrest'* (literally

* Himmler took it upon himself to approve and sign any application for this method of interrogation.

160

'sharp arrest', in other words a limited degree of torture).

But Pannwitz did neither. He saw that the man was in such a state of fear that he was ready to sing like a canary at any moment. For the time being he accepted Curda on his own terms. He knew about the briefcase. All right, then let him identify it first. Thereafter he would probe deeper. Check first, however, whether the man wasn't one of those crackpots that every investigation of this kind invariably turned up. An hour or so later Pannwitz was certain that he wasn't. He had identified the abandoned briefcase correctly, out of twenty others, by the tear in its side. In his report Pannwitz stated, 'His testimony . . . was immediately recognized as being an extremely important clue. . . . He had seen the briefcase before the assassination . . . then he had discovered that it contained an English sub-machine gun of a type he knew well.'

Now Curda really began to sing. He identified Kubis and Gabcik, names unknown to the Gestapo until that moment. Pannwitz realized that Curda must have been a para agent himself to know so much. He was strip-searched and the 'L' (for 'lethal') pill issued to British parachute agents was found on him.

Then they started to show the shaken Curda, who now realized that he had let himself in for more than he had expected, photos of suspects. Later Curda stated that he was beaten into identifying them, though in all probability he confessed of his own volition.

Pannwitz could hardly contain himself. They had made the initial breakthrough. Of all the millions of Czechs in that damned country, this wretch had fingered the handful they sought. But there was a catch. Curda didn't know where his fellow agents were hiding out. Still, Pannwitz was used to such things. It was all part and parcel of time-consuming police routine. Where had they been before the assassination, he asked. Curda started to give the addresses of the safe houses, knowing that as he did so he was condemning his fellow patriots to death. Still, it was only important to save his own neck now. One by one he gave away all the places used to hide fugitives by the Jindra group, in particular Auntie Marie's flat in Zizkov. It was the beginning of the end for those brave young men still hiding in the vaults of the church and all those who were aiding them.

It was a typical Gestapo *Nacht und Nebel* operation*: a knock on the door at five in the morning; the automobiles with their curtained rear windows drawn up ready and waiting; then sudden noise and clamour, angry shouts, the battering of rifle butts on the door. Moments later the policemen burst into the flat, threatening the half-dressed Auntie Marie and her son, Ata, with their pistols. The two were shoved against the wall while the cops went in search of her 'lodgers', but the birds had flown. Then Auntie Marie asked if she could go to the lavatory. She could. When she reappeared nobody noticed anything odd. Then she moaned, clutched at her stomach and slumped to the floor. She had taken cyanide.

Back at Gestapo HQ, Pannwitz grew nervous. He thought he had cracked the case after Curda's confession. Now all he had was the 21-year-old Ata. Reluctantly, but knowing that his own job was on the line, he ordered *'scharfer Arrest'*. The torture of Ata could begin.

All day long he was tortured in the cellars of the Pecek Palais. The Gestapo knew by now that the agents were being hidden in a Prague church, but the capital was full of churches. Which one was it? Besides, the Frank ultimatum was running out. They only had thirty-six hours left.

The interrogators redoubled their efforts, sensing that Ata really knew which was the church in question. At one point they filled him with cheap alcohol and then, horror of horrors, they brought in the severed head of his mother in a fish tank! They said that if he didn't speak they'd do the same to his father. In the end Ata gave in. He told his interrogators the name of the church. His mother had told him that if he were ever in serious trouble he should go to the catacombs beneath the St Cyril and Methodius Church. There he'd be safe. The fate of the agents was sealed.

---

* Night and Fog, ie. a secret operation in which the victim disappeared into the darkness, never to be seen again.

2

It was, in retrospect, remarkable how quickly the Party *Prominenz* seemed to forget the dead *Gruppenführer* after his state funeral. It seemed as if the bigshots heaved a collective sigh of relief that Heydrich was gone at last.

Bormann, the 'brown eminence' behind the Führer – 'anyone who wants access to the Führer has to go through *me*' – was obviously glad that he had vanished from the scene. Bormann knew that Heydrich had investigated his past and had compiled a dossier on his many affairs with the secretaries at the Führer's HQ. Gestapo Müller was another who was happy to see the back of the 'upstart'. Whoever took over Heydrich's post now would have to rely upon Müller for information on the intricacies of the state police apparatus. And it seemed as if Himmler shared Müller's point of view, for in due course he appointed the brutal Austrian lawyer Kaltenbrunner to replace Heydrich,* Schellenberg was another. Newly promoted to police and SS general, Heydrich's death cleared the way for him to play an independent role, without the 'dearly loved and missed Reinhard' breathing down his neck, and become Himmler's confidant.

Even Hitler, who seemed overcome and unable to say

---

* It is significant that so many Austrians, who after the war maintained that their country had been forcibly incorporated in the Nazi state, 'the Rape of Austria' as they called it, were key members of that state, from Hitler to Eichmann.

more than a few words at the state funeral, appeared only to remember him in anger at his stupidity in allowing himself to be killed the way he was. Thereafter he rarely made any reference to the man he had christened 'the man with the iron heart.'

His wife now appeared primarily concerned with how she would make ends meet. Who would look after her and the children? What would happen to the country house of which she was so proud, but which wasn't hers? A Czech, a former intimate of Dr Benes, promised to look after her affairs and said that if she had to flee one day she could leave her valuables with him and he would ensure their safety.* In the meantime she took up hunting in a big way. A strange form of hobby for a woman, one might think, but then her husband had been a 'hunter' for most of his adult life.

Even stranger was the attitude of his brother Thomas, at least in the eyes of his son, also called Thomas. Both had been present at the funeral of Uncle Reinhard, the father sticking out in 'his civilian clothes among all those uniforms', the son proud in his Hitler Youth outfit. Shortly thereafter, as the son recalls, 'A strange SS officer appeared at our house in Berlin with some personal papers of Reinhards for my father. He locked himself in his room all night to read them and in the morning he burned them. Why, he never said. Although he hadn't needed to do so, he volunteered for the front, after being engaged in some mysterious anti-Nazi activities. I couldn't understand it. I was a fervent disciple of the Führer and proud of being a junior member of the Hitler Youth. In October, 1944, my father disappeared at the front, declared "missing, believed killed". He never came back. But, why he went I don't know to this day.'

By now Pannwitz had taken up his headquarters in the vaults of the Petschek Bank from where he would direct the operation

* He didn't. They disappeared at the end of the war, never to reappear. But Frau Heydrich did manage to take Reinhard's death mask, his uniform and the silver baptismal platter given to him on the occasion of the birth of his first child by no less a person than Captain Roehm, 'liquidated' as head of the SA by Hitler.

against the agents hidden in the church. At the same time Gestapo men were on their way to arrest the churchmen in Resslova Street. Some seven hundred SS men of the Prague garrison had been alerted to follow up the arrests by an all-out attack on the church, if necessary.

Pannwitz worked from his large-scale map of the area pinned on the wall. The SS would first seal off the area, so there would be no escape. He pointed out windows, doors and rooftops where the SS marksmen would be stationed to pick off anyone who tried to make a run for it.

Then, once everyone was in place, the assault would go in. Pannwitz had even found an expert guide, a Herr Streiber of the Prague police, who would lead the first SS men through the back door. There they hoped to find a churchman with all the many keys used in such an ancient church.

Finally, Pannwitz warned them that there might well be a secret passage leading from the catacombs to the river, and that both Himmler and Hitler were awaiting the out-come. Nobody had better slip up or there would be serious trouble.

Now it was up to SS General von Treuenfeld who had the overall command of the fighting troops. He would send in the first group of SD and SS men. Their orders were to take the killers alive if possible. The Führer wanted a show trial by which to demonstrate what heartless troublemakers the Czech leaders in exile and their British bosses were. But it would never come to that.

Still the seven agents slept or kept watch – three above and four below. Tomorrow they were to move. Prague had become too hot for them. In the morning they were going to be taken to a new hiding place in the country. It would be easier to get them to safety from there, or so they had been told.

Kubis was the first to sound the alarm. He warned his comrades, Opalka and Svarc, that something strange was going on outside. It was about dawn and they crept to their well-rehearsed positions, prepared to fight it out.

Kubis was right. He had heard something. It was the sound of muffled jackboots heading down the corridor which led to the priests' quarters. But the SS found no one except a sleepy janitor who complained at being woken at that time of the morning. However, the look on the Germans' faces soon changed his tune and he produced his keys and started opening doors. The searchers spread out in all directions, flashing their torches in dusty nooks and crannies, pulling aside drab curtains, and peering into corners. Nothing. There was no sign of the expected paras.

Then Pannwitz arrived on the scene and started snapping out orders. He wanted the killers alive. They had to be hidden somewhere. Surely they hadn't been able to break through his cordon already.

A locked door with a metal grille leading from the choir couldn't be opened.

'*Wo ist der Schluessel?*' Pannwitz demanded. The janitor hadn't got one. Pannwitz didn't hesitate. '*Aufbrechen!*' he ordered and the SS started to force the grille open with the butts of their guns. The grille swung open and almost immediately they heard the bouncing rattle of something metal on the floor. As the grenade burst there followed the angry chatter of a sub-machine gun at close range. Slugs whined off the stone and shards flew everywhere.

On the roofs around the church the SS now started blasting away. The dawn calm was destroyed by the sudden racket. Windows were shattered. Smoke and dust rose on all sides. The altar hangings went up in flames. The interior of the church glowed a dull orange. Pannwitz yelled above the racket that his squad should withdraw while there was still time. Otherwise they might be slaughtered by their own side.

After several minutes order was restored. A squad of SS men went rushing in to storm the choir loft. They were to take the assassins alive if they could. There would be no more indiscriminate shooting. But it wasn't as easy as Pannwitz thought. The SS had to advance up a narrow circular staircase. It was one of those places where one man and a boy could hold off a whole regiment if they were determined enough – and the Czechs were determined. What had they to hope for save death? If that was the case, they'd make as many Huns as possible pay the price.

Bullets whined off the walls. The SS ducked, fired, edged

166

their way upwards. But they were paying for the ground they gained. Pannwitz told their officer to send up reinforcements and finally they reached the landing. Here the going was easier, but not much. Still the Czechs remained defiant. Outnumbered as they were and running low on ammunition, they continued to keep their attackers at bay.

The SS started pulling stick grenades out of the cloth bags slung around their necks and flinging them to their front, advancing behind this rough-and-ready 'artillery barrage'. The tactic proved successful. Besides, they had superiority in numbers – a whole squad against three, with limited ammunition. While Pannwitz sheltered anxiously below, they battled forward. For two hours the fight continued, but finally the noise of the Sten guns began to die away, while the heavy thud of the German Schmeisser machine pistols continued until the noise was all one-sided. From above a voice cried, '*Alles in Ordnung,*' followed by the order, 'Cease firing'.

Pannwitz hurried up to the roof. The place was a shambles. Rubble and shattered laths lay everywhere. He crunched across a carpet of empty cartridge cases to where the weary SS men were warily turning over bodies with their boots. 'How many?' he asked.

'Three,' came the answer. Just three men had held them up for a good two hours. Then, when it had seemed hopeless and their ammunition had begun to run low, they had swallowed the cyanide pills they had brought from England. Two had died at once. The third, Kubis, was still half-conscious. According to Pannwitz's latter statement, 'He had tried to use poison, but had apparently lost consciousness. He was immediately transferred to hospital, but none of the doctors' attempts to keep him alive succeeded. He died within twenty minutes.'

3

The SS men shoved the bearded preacher, Vladimir Petrek, in front of Pannwitz, standing there in the rubble of the now silent church. The priest was afraid, Pannwitz could see that, but he was bearing up well. After all, he was going to die, in his case probably under the blade of the guillotine. He showed the priest a coat his men had found and said it was proof that there was another 'treacherous killer' hidden somewhere in the church. Where was he? Petrek knew he had no choice. He led them to the entrance to the catacombs. As von Treuenfeld wrote in his report: 'There was a stone lid, beneath which there was a ladder leading to the cellar. The head of the Czech Fire Brigade, who we had brought along with us on account of his expertise in such matters, said it would take three to four hours to move the lid, so we ordered the priest to tell the criminals below to surrender. He did so. their answer came back clearly, "*Never*". Thereupon we sealed up the place the best we could and the fire brigade started to pump in water and a choking gas. But the water level rose only slowly. We concluded from that that there was a tunnel leading away from below, through which the water drained and through which the criminals might well yet escape.'

The Germans had to try something else. A volunteer troop of the SS Regiment *Deutschland* was whistled up. The fire brigade was ordered to stop pumping water into the cellar and the SS advanced. They had almost reached their target when they came under fire. The officer in charge of the assault troop forgot Pannwitz's order to try to take the Czechs alive and ordered his men to return the unseen agents' fire.

In the meantime, in another section of the underground rooms, the priest pleaded with the resisters through a grille to give in. To no avail. Curda and Ata were then dragged up. Curda appealed to the cornered men: 'Surrender, boys. Everything will be all right.' His answer was a burst of fire from the defenders. Ata, defiant to the last, refused to help the Germans and was dragged away as Pannwitz ordered the Czech fire brigade to flood the crypt.

It seems to be typical of how much Heydrich had cowed the Czechs that one of them climbed up a ladder, braving possible fire from his trapped compatriots hidden below, knocked off the lid of a grille, directed a fire hose inside and started to pump in two thousand litres of water a minute in an attempt to flood the crypt and force the defenders to surrender. But the Czechs of the fire brigade mistook the courage of the agents. They knew they were doomed one way or another, but still they fought on. Splashing through the knee-deep water, they placed a short ladder against the wall inside and clambered up, fighting the powerful jets, and started to cut the hose.

As von Treuenfeld wrote in his report: 'The *Waffen SS* were then ordered to throw tear-gas grenades down the shaft. . . . However, the criminals often managed to throw them back. Hoses were again put into the shaft. A few hand grenades were used this time to stop the criminals pushing the hoses out again.'

By now Karl Frank had arrived on the scene. This battle in the middle of the city was, he felt, ruining Germany's reputation. The Czechs had to be dealt with *immediately*. It was a viewpoint with which von Treuenfeld agreed. The Czechs were making a laughing stock of the SS. 'What did the Gestapo know of war?' he asked. Why should these damned Czechs be taken alive? Pannwitz retorted that his men could have captured them *dead* six hours ago, but they were needed for the show trial to come.

Then Frank took over. The Czechs had to be taken *now*. It was a matter of prestige. If they were killed in the attempt, what did it matter? Pannwitz knew that Frank and the SS General outranked him. *He* had done his best. Let them get on with it. The blood bath could begin.

The events of the next hour or so, the last that the four brave Czechs spent on this earth, are somewhat confused, which is to be expected under the circumstances. Even the SS had become nervous and jumpy. It was said that Frank and Treuenfeld couldn't find any volunteers to make the final attack, but in the end a soldier did volunteer and then the rest fell in. All were heavily armed with grenades, pistols and their usual rifles, plus, ironically enough, two soldiers with the new top-secret automatic assault rifles specially developed at the Skoda Works for the SS!

Now, according to von Treuenfeld, a brief firefight took place. Other reports maintain that, even before the SS reluctantly attacked, the inevitable happened. Four shots echoed from below and a man was sent down to find out what had happened. *'Fertig!'* he shouted back. The Czechs were finished.

According to von Treuenfeld's report: 'Four dead criminals were found in the crypt. Apart from serious injuries, they had wounds in the temple showing that they had killed themselves with their own revolvers.'

The corpses were then dragged from the church and thrown on to the pavement outside where Curda was waiting to identify them. He walked along the line, with German Army cameramen waiting to record the event so that audiences all over Occupied Europe would learn of the retribution that would descend upon them if they resisted the will of their conquerors. Then Curda identified Gabcik.

At that moment a messenger from *Reichsführer SS* Himmler arrived. He seemed like a character from a Shakespeare play bearing a missive from the monarch. The message he bore read: 'Any means should be employed to reassure the assassins in order to capture them alive.' Pannwitz shrugged as it was read aloud to Frank, who had forgotten his reading glasses. But, as far as Frank was concerned, the case was closed. He'd be glad to get back to Berlin. So they went their various ways to celebrate, to contemplate, to mourn.

But Pannwitz was not yet quite finished with the Czechs. He

was assigned to wind up the Prague underground, while the Gestapo went further afield, shooting the families of the dead agents as a matter of routine. Vanek and the surviving Sokol members were arrested and the Professor was interrogated by Pannwitz. In his report he remarked that the Professor was typically middle-class and was worried about a communist takeover of his homeland if Germany lost the war. Not that Germany would, he hastened to add, as if Pannwitz might be offended by his reference to defeat. But Pannwitz had been a cop under the Kaiser, the Weimar Republic and now under Hitler. As he used to tell his old cronies, 'I'll still be a cop even if old Uncle Joe takes over.' Like any sensible man, his main concern was surviving and finally enjoying his pension.

According to Pannwitz' statement, 'Jindra did not feel that the Allies should put the Czech nation at risk for their war aims after having deserted her in 1938 and 1939. Besides, the strength of the German Army was so great that the Germans would not hesitate to use any means to keep the Protectorate in their hands. Unrest or revolt would be suicide for the Czech people.'

Vanek's attitude was to cause dismay in London when it reached there. But he had hit the nail on the head, and in a way he was still sticking to an essential truth when he collaborated with the Germans by identifying already arrested resistance workers and urging them to confess as he had done. All the Jews, Czechs, Slovaks and others who had died at German hands after Heydrich's murder had done so in the interest of a cold-hearted *realpolitik*.

But had that sacrifice served the purpose which Benes had intended? President Roosevelt had toyed with the idea of calling the new conflict 'the War of the Tyrants', but after a while he had given up the idea and settled for the more mundane 'World War Two'. Heydrich had been the only German tyrant to be punished by death in that war. But it had served no useful purpose. The Czech people had *not* revolted, although five thousand of their countrymen had been killed by the Nazis. There had been no mass go slow in the German-run war industries. Indeed, production had increased and right to the end the Skoda Works were turning out very effective self-propelled guns for the *Wehrmacht*. SOE calculated that sixty-five percent of the Czech population were still co-operating with the Germans in the remaining years of the war. Polish Intelligence actually put it as high as eighty percent.

Death had come to the tyrant admittedly, but it hadn't changed the nature of the war one iota.

AFTERMATH

There are no memorials to Reinhard Tristan Heydrich in Germany, or elsewhere for that matter, today. Naturally the ones erected by the Nazis in Prague in 1943 were torn down in May, 1945, after the SS sent to guard the 'holy shrine' had run for their lives. There is still extant a stamp with his death mask on it, the highest value ever issued by the *Reichspost*. Some said at the time that it would be a collectors' item. They were wrong. That death mask, beautiful yet chilling, put the collectors off.

Unlike Hess, Skorzeny and Peiper, the hero-criminals of the Third Reich who still have a coterie of followers and 'fans' over half a century later, Heydrich never attracted a following. No pilgrims ever went to visit his wife and children on that remote North German island where she ran a snack bar.

Hitler has his autobahns, the monumental buildings in Munich, Nuremberg and elsewhere, even that vaunted *Westwall* the Siegfried Line, which still remind the world, if it wants to be reminded, of *Der Führer des Grossdeutschen Reichs*, not Heydrich. Neither in deed nor in stone is there anything left to recall him.

Save perhaps one thing. That long winding trail of gold, hidden and then refound, wending its way from country to country, from continent to continent, greedily sought after and frantically defended, hidden in underground bank chambers for decades until its guardians almost forgot it existed – that shining link between the evil empire of the 'New Order' in the discredited past and the 'New Europe' of the twenty-first century created indirectly by Heydrich's successors. Does that trail really exist? Are past, present and future inextricably linked, cemented together by evil and murder?

Perhaps the American novelist Scott Fitzgerald summed up the link between past and present best. In *The Great Gatsby* he wrote of the dead Gatsby who might, in another life, have been called 'Gatz' (a supposedly Jewish name): 'Gatsby believed in the green light, the orgiastic future that year by year recedes before us. It eluded us then, but that's no matter – tomorrow we will run faster, stretch out our arms further. . . . So we beat on, boats against the current, borne back ceaselessly into the past.'

INDEX